PIERRE BOURGAULT

TRANSLATED BY DAVID HOMEL

NOW or NeveR!

MANIFESTO

FOR AN

INDEPENDENT

QUEBEC

KEY PORTER BOOKS

Canadian Cataloguing in Publication Data

Bourgault, Pierre, 1934-
    Now or never!
Translation of: Maintenant ou jamais!
ISBN 1-55013-315-2

1. Quebec (Province) - History - Autonomy and independence
movements.   2. Canada - Constitutional law - Amendments.
3. Federal-provincial relations - Canada.*   I. Title.

FC2925.9.S37B68 1991   971.4'04   C91-093315-4
F1053.2.B68 1991

Key Porter Books Limited
70 The Esplanade
Toronto, Ontario
Canada M5E 1R2

Printed and bound in Canada

91 92 93 94 95 6 5 4 3 2 1

For Jacques Parizeau, in tribute

Contents

Preface to the English Edition

When I finished this book, at the end of August in 1990, I was quite sure that we were witnessing an unprecedented acceleration of history.

It so happens that I was right to a certain extent. As a matter of fact, things have accelerated even faster than I had imagined.

It means that by the time you read this book, at least some parts may already be obsolete.

But this book being about movement, I decided not to change anything.

It may be difficult to feel this movement outside of Quebec, but I can assure you that it is tremendous. One should be aware of it if only to try to understand what will happen in the next few years.

This book is also about probability. If things go on accelerating the way they are now, Quebec may be independent before you have finished reading it.

Introduction

Now or never!

There are some rendezvous with history that you just shouldn't miss.

We missed one in 1980, and we came close to missing out for a long, long time to come. I'm not the only one who didn't expect this historical opportunity to come again for another 30 or 40 years or, worse, never again.

But we're lucky. Extraordinarily lucky. Here we are, faced with political circumstances so exceptional we can scarcely believe our eyes.

Who would have thought, a scant two years ago, that the independence movement in Quebec would not only come alive again, but would, according to all the polls and all the forecasts, receive a majority of popular support from Quebec voters?

Of course, we shouldn't count our chickens before they're hatched. It might be that the enthusiasm we've been witnessing over the past few months will subside for no apparent reason, or dissipate with no hope of return.

We have to be cautious. But caution does not mean sitting quietly on the sidelines, waiting for events to sort themselves out. On the contrary. We have to make events happen.

In the 1970s, we got bogged down in strategies that were complicated and often contradictory. Strategies, rather than means, became the goal. Analyses that were supposedly the most advanced had a way of forgetting power relations and tough political realities.

Strategies and analyses were too often a pretext for our whimpering hesitation, a pitiful mask for our fears. They provided the illusion that we were moving ahead; in reality, we were running in place. They drowned objectives and priorities in the fathomless well of private will and personal choice.

Finally, we actually forgot the goal we had set for ourselves. We took off in every direction at once, and got nowhere.

It wouldn't be hard to fall into the same traps again. Everyone has his own particular idea on what tomorrow's Quebec should be and on how to get there.

Nickel-and-dime strategies that we thought had disappeared altogether are on the loose again, busy creating new scenarios and introducing new steps.

That's dangerous. We could miss the boat again. But this time, we won't be able to plead ignorance.

If we want to avoid yesterday's pitfalls, we must never lose sight of our objective, and we must remind all those willing to listen to us just what it is.

The objective? For more than 30 years, it's been the independence of Quebec.

I feel a little ridiculous having to state it again. But when I think of all the detours we took, and all the contorted positions we assumed to avoid talking about it, or to put off its arrival, I know I have to keep hitting at that point, at the risk of repeating myself.

The fuzzy concept of sovereignty-association has reared its head. Robert Bourassa's superstructures clutter the landscape. There are more and more proposals for defining a renewed Canada. Naive and dubious alliances are made in a bandwagon atmosphere, and many people are rushing off in every direction at once, pursuing personal priorities, without any mandate or authority.

That's the context. And that's why I have to repeat a few things that everyone knows, so that our objective doesn't get drowned in the murky waters of a certain Lake.

At the same time, there's an urgency to the situation. That's why I say we have to act now or never.

I don't like that expression very much. There is something definitive about it that doesn't correspond to historical movements and the moods of a nation.

The "never" bothers me. The same can't be said for the "now."

I feel very deeply that the time for action is now. The turn of events has never been so favourable. For the first time in my life, I feel I can say with no exaggeration: I just might see independence in my lifetime.

I know I'm not the only one with that feeling.

Today, everything is coming together to give the independence position the upper hand. Even if the battle is far from over, it would be unpardonable not to add our strongest efforts to the peaceful enthusiasm shown by the Quebec people for some time now.

In history, things happen when there is a conjunction between players and movements.

The situation might be favourable, but if no one can make use of events, nothing will happen. That was the case in France in 1968. There was a veritable revolutionary situation. Everyone recognized it; no one denied it. But no one could carry that movement into power. The French Communist Party could have seized the moment but, outmoded, full of internal struggles and criticized from the outside, it had to settle for the role of spectator.

On the other hand, the "revolutionaries" found themselves at the head of a spontaneous movement that was bigger than they were. With no adequate organization or sufficient structure, they had to settle for displaying their anger before de Gaulle who, once he got over his shock, recovered his mastery of the situation and used it to reinforce his power.

The contrary may occur, too. Players without a movement.

Perhaps that's what happened in Quebec in 1980. The players were present: a strong party holding the reins of power in Quebec, the Parti québécois, solid and experienced party workers, adequate structures.

But apparently, the movement was not strong enough. The adversary's strength, sorely underestimated, broke it down in no time.

Things seem different today.

The main opponent is on the canvas. Ottawa and English Canada have been KOed, and it'll take them some time before they're back on their feet again.

The players, though scattered, are more numerous than ever. It wouldn't take much for them to come together in a powerful organization.

The movement can be felt all the way to the street. Opinion polls keep telling us that people are moving, and they're going in the direction we want.

There seems to be a conjunction between the players and the movement.

That state of affairs never lasts very long. The people get tired, and the players like to change roles.

That's why I say it's time to act now. That's why I say it's now or never.

Once again, I am going to try to clear the land, define what's at stake, and suggest some ways we might reach our goal.

I don't possess the truth. But I think my instincts are good.

If I'm right — and contrary to habit, this time I hope I'm not wrong — if I'm right, we have reached a kind of crossroads.

Intersections are always dangerous. They can cause confusion. Which is why I want to set down a few signposts and guidelines.

This book is informed by a feeling of urgency. I wrote it in the same wave of feeling that moves the *québécois* people and that has always been my lifeblood.

I wrote it at white heat, as the events were taking place, and the situation changed daily. I might be ahead of myself at certain times, and behind at other times. Sometimes, I hope, I'll hit the bull's-eye.

I wrote this book fast and hard, to reach the deadline.

Because we'll have to act fast and hard to meet the deadline ourselves.

Because it's NOW or NEVER!

PART ONE
The Stage Is Set

"Do you remember the day we really started moving again, back in 1990? I remember it well."

That's how I ended my last book, in April of 1989.

To support my beliefs, I used a few vague feelings I had at the time, a few hints I'd gotten. But I never thought I'd be a prophet.

Things have moved so fast in the meantime that I can hardly catch my breath.

I never thought we'd be here today. Everyone agrees: the political juncture has never been so favourable for us.

But just what is a political juncture?

It's the sum of the events, circumstances, public opinion swings, feelings of necessity, and deep and sometimes unspoken desires.

A positive political juncture occurs when all these elements come together in a given space and time. The juncture creates a movement towards one objective, and away from another.

Today, the situation is favourable to the objective of Quebec sovereignty. Independence-minded people aren't the only ones talking about the juncture. Jean Chrétien can't imagine a favourable climate for his option — his obsession — until the day every Quebecker will have gazed upon the Rocky Mountains.

A favourable situation cannot be brought into being by decree. It exists or it doesn't. Then we have to be able to recognize it. In this particular case, there's no shortage of signs.

Consensus: One or Many?

Several months ago, there was talk about the consensus beginning to develop in Quebec. What consensus? What was it about? No one had the answer. It was all rather vague.

After the failure of the Meech Lake Accord, people stopped talking about a developing consensus. They shifted over to a solid, articulated, real consensus.

Everyone nodded their heads and took note, in Quebec and elsewhere, and the consensus became part of the landscape.

People talked about this consensus as if it were the latest crop of blueberries from Lac Saint-Jean. "They're big and juicy this year, and there're plenty of them."

The harvest will be good.

The consensus looks promising.

But what exactly are we harvesting? No one knows, but it doesn't matter, as long as there's a consensus. It's just another way of going in circles, but people like saying the word.

In reality, there is no true consensus. There are tendencies, movements, statements that seem to come together, major turning points, polls that might suggest that . . . there's something in the air.

That something — let's call it tension — should not be confused with true consensus.

There's quite a distance between tension and the solid backing of a majority of citizens that creates consensus.

Whatever the case may be, none of that is important, since the perception we have of reality is often more important than the reality itself.

Therefore, if we "perceive" a consensus, we can maintain that it exists. That's what we're all doing, without worrying about digging deeper to discover the truth.

Perception helps the spread of a favourable juncture. The perception may be true, it may be false, but that matters little. Because now, a good number of people who once believed they were in the minority see themselves as having been catapulted into the majority.

Success breeds success. When an idea appears to be gaining momentum, the unbelievers convert, the doubters find strength to believe, and the cowards begin to shake their fists.

The appearance of consensus can create a dynamic that actually leads to a real consensus.

The idea of Quebec sovereignty has been making progress in people's minds. The idea is still vague for many citizens, but at least it has stopped frightening them. That in itself is a major victory.

The situation is favourable for supporters of sovereignty. Buoyed by the mood of the times, they can advance their ideas without fear of a shower of rotten eggs.

No movement is irreversible. But when a situation is favourable, the movement gathers momentum and we begin to feel nothing can stop it.

Bill 178 and Quebec Youth

I detected the first signs of the movement, some two years ago, among young people.

We were still bogged down in the post-Referendum blues. Most people who had fought for independence gazed upon their broken dreams, bitterness and contained despair in their hearts.

The atmosphere is called lethargy.

I didn't feel like celebrating any more than anyone else.

I hadn't been invited to speak at a college or high school for nearly eight years. It had become axiomatic that young people were apolitical, that our sons and daughters were concerned solely with personal success. Not surprising, considering the example we had set them.

But many young people were having thoughts and feelings unknown to us. In almost an underground way, they were preparing themselves for future struggles.

I received one invitation, then another. Then 10, then 40.

The first invitations came from students who attended schools in which the majority of the student body was of immigrant background. More often than not, English was the language used. Powerless, French-speaking students did not know where to turn.

They defended themselves as best they could. But with no resources and no structure, they were taking two steps back for every one they took forward.

Some of the more determined students had begun creating committees to defend French — that's right, in our so-called French schools! — and that's when they had the idea to invite me to speak to them about both language and sovereignty.

I was surprised at how receptive they were.

They knew almost nothing about the rhetoric of independence. But they loved hearing it, as if it provided them with the beginnings of an answer to their dilemma.

In every school, I discovered the same atmosphere, the same serene and peaceful enthusiasm, the same curiosity and determination.

Could it be, I asked myself, still doubting, that we are witnessing the rebirth of something that strangely resembles the dreams of our youth? I was as careful in the answer to that question as I was loath to actually ask it.

Deep down, I didn't want to believe it.

A few months later, the National Assembly adopted Bill 178. The movement was on, once and for all.

On one side were the English, who claimed they were being persecuted. On the other side were those who thought they'd been cheated.

Suddenly, the invitations came pouring in. And they weren't coming only from schools with immigrant majorities. They came from all over Montreal, and from outside the city, where all the faces were white and all the words spoken in French.

There was action there like everywhere else. Once again, I was surprised to see that young people were fighting for their language as if the movement had never stopped.

Their struggles were not the same as ours. Thirty years earlier, we had fought to give French the role it should always have had in a society in which English was omnipresent, an outrageously dominating force.

Our campaign had partially succeeded. Our children were able to grow up in a much more French society than the one we had known. They weren't fighting to conquer what they didn't have; their struggle was to maintain the gains made.

We had fought to win back our language. They were fighting to keep it.

Right or wrong, they felt that Bill 178 stripped them of what they believed was their natural prerogative, their inalienable right.

They were thrilled to discover the rhetoric of independence.

And they began influencing the blasé old politicos who had brought them into this world, the ones they had dinner with when they came back from school.

That's how it came to pass that some 60,000 of these discouraged middle-aged types, in the company of their children, took to the streets one day in Montreal to protest against Bill 178. The largest demonstration of all time.

Something really was happening.

Well . . . maybe. Well . . . I think so. Well . . . but is it for real? Well . . . I hope so. Well . . . it's too soon to tell.

I wasn't sure. I hesitated. I hoped the whole thing wasn't just a flash in the pan.

I was afraid of disappointment. I opted for caution.

Still, I was hopeful. I figured that if young people were starting to move, everything could change. The movement could get a second wind. The battle, the one we thought we had lost, would be on again.

The movement among young people was the first sign I had that the situation was turning in our favour.

That doesn't constitute proof, I know. But it was more solid than I'd thought at the time.

From then on, things started gathering speed at an almost frenetic pace, and soon we reached the situation we are seeing today.

I'm not claiming that young people created the situation. But they did provide the first element.

The Parti Québécois

Two or three years ago, the Parti québécois had all but disappeared. More than 80 percent of its members had quit after René Lévesque's catastrophic *beau risque* policy, or betting on federal renewal. And what was left had no relation to an authentically pro-sovereignty party.

The Société Saint-Jean-Baptiste and the Société nationale des Québécois held the fort as best they could, while a small number of sovereignty supporters gravitated towards a few lifeless political groups.

In conditions like these, it's difficult, if not impossible, to try to assemble the troops and urge them to cross what seems at the time like an endless desert.

Then things began to change quickly. Jacques Parizeau took charge of the Parti québécois and announced his intentions: the Parti québécois would return to its true nature and make Quebec sovereignty its absolute priority.

The results were felt immediately. Thousands of former party workers returned to the front lines, while others signed up for the first time.

Enthusiastic meetings and conventions confirmed its rebirth as the party of independence.

There was a world to win. And that's exactly what Jacques Parizeau set out to do with the help of his co-workers who, this time, were happy to be fighting once more for the cause.

To recover its credibility, the Parti québécois decided to pick up where it had left off around 1975. It had to return to its roots, its motivating force: promoting Quebec independence.

Which is what it did. Timidly at first, then more vigorously during the 1989 provincial election.

It was a last-chance election. Either the Parti québécois, having shown its true colours, would get wiped out, its "rebirth" destroyed in the process, or it would succeed in maintaining its position, strengthening it if possible, then move on to greater things.

With Jacques Parizeau as leader, the Parti québécois fought a good hard campaign. When the dust settled, it was once again solidly ensconced in the National Assembly and in the minds of the electorate.

Quebec's instrument of independence had not only survived years of internal sabotage, it was united as never before, its policies more coherent and its workers ready for action.

Nationalist feelings in Quebec were only just beginning to stir from their slumber. But at least this time, should they wake up, they wouldn't be faced with an institutional void and the scattering of individual political energies.

As I said, when the situation is favourable, if something is to happen, you must have an organization present that can seize the occasion.

Though the juncture still wasn't very positive, at least an organization was present at a strategic point: as Opposition in the National Assembly. The movement had a structure now and the direction was clear to everyone.

We might ask ourselves whether the nationalist feelings stirring Quebec today would have been as strong if the Parti québécois hadn't undergone its rebirth and shown that, despite the sceptics, the idea was still alive, and that Quebeckers still wanted to hear the language of independence.

Personally, I don't think so. But whatever the case, what was done was done well, and the Parti québécois is now part of the sense of a positive political juncture.

The Business Class

I think it would be fair to say that, over the last two years, business people in Quebec have had a decisive role in the juncture.

I deplore the influence they have on our society. I don't deny their success and I'm happy for them. But I fear and mistrust them because, most of the time, they can't see any farther than the end of their nose — which usually means their own particular interests at the time.

They have trouble with long-term thinking, and an even harder time considering collective interests.

That being said, I don't see why I'd snub them if they wanted to offer me their help.

To tell the truth, they're the ones who sounded the alarm nearly two years ago, at the time of the Meech Lake affair. No one cared much about it; it wasn't a subject of discussion. Meech Lake was a far-off, rather abstract issue until the business class got together to support the Accord in its entirety. Mr. Bourassa had said that Quebec's five conditions were non-negotiable, without exception. He settled for repeating his line, but he never went any further.

For a while, the business class followed his lead. Then they began making threats. "If the Accord isn't passed, the Canadian economy will suffer."

People started listening.

Someone went a little further. "If English Canada doesn't want us, we can get along alone very well indeed."

Suddenly there was an explosion. A kind of competition for the most startling statement:

"Independence doesn't frighten the business class any more."

"Quebec has a strong, diversified economy. If we have to, we'll go it alone."

"Sovereignty may be the natural outcome of the evolution of Quebec society."

"Not necessarily independence, but independence if necessary."

"Canada has more to lose than Quebec."

And that's only a sampling.

Up until then, not a single businessman had come out categorically in favour of Quebec sovereignty. Independence was a last-resort solution, a kind of worst-case scenario. We have to be wary of rhetoric that discusses independence through a negative approach. "If they don't want us . . ." Well, it doesn't make any difference whether they want us or not. You don't choose independence for or against others; you do it for yourself. It's a value in itself. Independence isn't reaction; it's action.

Even though the statements coming out of the financial centres on the rue Saint-Jacques were far from being a solemn engagement towards Quebec sovereignty, people felt that something was changing on that street.

It was becoming obvious that the Quebec business class had achieved a degree of self-confidence. They trusted their own means. They were sure of themselves, and they wouldn't be had through blackmail as easily as in the past.

The people weren't mistaken. In these declarations, they saw a kind of exorcism of all the fears that had haunted them for so long. And since the people trust the business class almost blindly, they are often quick to follow them, no questions asked.

It was easy to go from that position to a conclusion that independence would not be a catastrophe, and that it might even contain something positive.

At least, we knew one thing. If the choice had to be made between independence and federalism, the business class would not line up against sovereignty, as they had before. They might not go down to the Montreal Forum to applaud Jacques Parizeau, but at least they'd remain neutral.

In a society that has had such trouble throwing off its inferiority complex in economic matters, the declarations of the business class had a spectacular effect.

Nationalist fever climbed a notch.

Members of the business class themselves, as if caught in their own trap, were astonished to discover that they were a lot more nationalist than they had suspected. Pushed by their statements, the situation made giant steps. The surprise of it all only added to the effect.

Over the last ten years, feelings had ripened into fullness. Embers had smouldered under the ashes. No one had noticed until, suddenly, the fire was alive again.

That fire threw a whole new light on the situation.

The Americans

The Quebec business class went a long way towards reassuring the population. But there was another tenacious fear we couldn't shake off: the fear of the Americans.

Sharing a border with the United States, Quebec would certainly be the first to suffer if ever the Americans decided to reject the idea of sovereignty.

Over the last 30 years, I've heard this fear discussed over and over again, even among the most committed militants. It is not an unreasonable fear. We know the strength of the Americans; we are acquainted with their violent reactions and quick tempers. No one is blind to their intransigence and the brutal way they have of protecting their interests.

Besides, we are in what they call their sphere of influence. Sure, we're afraid. Ours is a healthy fear.

That fear surfaced and threatened the juncture that seemed to be improving day by day. But things were about to change there, too.

First came Jean-François Lisée's book, *In the Eye of the Eagle*. Lisée is a talented writer, and in the book he describes the relations over the past 30 years between Quebec and the United States. Surprise, surprise! The Americans, including the most powerful among them, display no ferocious hostility towards sovereignty. Most of them are against it, but not aggressively so. In other words, they would prefer Quebec to remain in Confederation but, if that does not turn out to be the case, they'll get along very well with whatever happens.

We even encountered a few Americans who were in favour of sovereignty. The most astonishing discovery was that the Americans are much better informed than we thought, and that they don't see Quebec as an under-developed country. They haven't detected any virulent anti-American feelings in Quebec; quite the opposite is true. In Quebec, pro-American feeling is probably stronger than in the rest of Canada.

To my surprise, I discovered that they judged me to be "pragmatic." Delighted, I informed my friends of this — who immediately dissolved in peals of laughter.

Lisée's book went its merry way. But, as usual, it never touched the masses.

Around that time, major American newspapers began running a series of articles giving Quebec a much more positive image, in contrast to the past. They discussed Quebec independence in calmer tones, and in some cases, even in a sympathetic manner.

American journalists trotted out figures to show that Quebec could get along alone if necessary, displaying the economic strength of its little northern neighbour.

No one talked about sending in the Marines the day Quebec declared its independence. No threats, no blackmail, no hints of aggression.

The tone was more striking than the content. The ogre might not be as fearsome as we had always thought.

In a lot of people's minds, if the Americans would "let" us have independence without invading the country, then anything was possible. The final barrier fell. Fear dissipated; the world opened up.

Quebec media hurried to reproduce, in an advantageous position, all these articles flowing in from our neighbour to the south. They were analysed and commented upon, and their impact increased.

Echoes are louder in a little room. Besides being fearful, Quebeckers don't want to offend anyone . . . especially the Americans.

Now it was turning out that the Americans were taking the whole thing calmly. They weren't talking about a "Cuba of the North." They would go on investing here if it was in their interest to do so, and they would keep on teaching French in their schools.

God bless America!

In July 1990, newspapers reported that the New England states would continue buying Quebec electricity, whether or not we became independent. The frosting on the cake!

What more could we want?

The situation was building in our favour.

Opinion Polls

Opinion polls, like the media, can magnify trends as they report on them.

Why? Because everyone wants to be on the winning team, in fashion, on the right side, reassured of their existence.

Opinion polls don't create opinion; they reflect it at a moment in time. Sometimes, they reflect what turns out to be capricious trends. But if they detect deep-seated opinions that hold through from one poll to the next, that's when they begin influencing the minds of the population.

Over this last year, almost every poll uncovered a very clear progression in support for Quebec sovereignty. Support soon passed the 50 percent mark to reach 70 percent at certain points.

Immediately reported and broadcast by the newspapers, television, and radio, these figures proved comforting for the pro-independence side, while shaking up the un-decided and increasing the legions of the converted.

It's the same old story: the bandwagon effect.

It holds true for any kind of opinion, for any behaviour or product consumption.

People are social. They like to be on the side of the majority.

What is the influence of opinion polls on the current situation? They showed that a clear majority of Quebeckers support sovereignty for the first time in 30 years.

That in itself didn't change the situation. But the opinion polls, added to other elements of the political juncture, supported and solidified it.

Everything makes sense. If the polls showed only 27 percent in favour of sovereignty, Robert Bourassa would make sweeping statements against it and, by that fact, prevent the movement from making progress. If the polls revealed 63 percent for sovereignty, Bourassa would not become a separatist, but at least he wouldn't make any impetuous statements against that possibility. He would even pretend to open the door to it. And in so doing, he would contribute to the movement's growth.

If the movement grows, workers will fight harder and change more people's minds. If the number of the con-verted grows, advertising and marketing agencies will want to serve this new clientele by giving it a greater flavour of independence.

And the media, which has a duty to reflect public opin-ion, will put the poll results on page one.

And so forth and so on . . .

The political juncture is made up of these smaller elements that, when put together, define more or less favourable conditions for a given possibility.

The Media

Did the media play a determining role in the creation of the current situation? I don't think so.

Media don't create political situations. They only accompany and reflect them.

However, if they don't do their job, if the information doesn't get through, if analyses are not made, if commentary is not to the point, the population will obviously have a harder time recognizing itself and synthesizing the elements that have led to the political juncture. The population might not be able to deal itself into the situation.

Over the past few years, I've often heard people complain that they're not receiving quality information. They criticize the media for not supplying what's necessary to help them make an informed decision. When you push them a little, you realize they should really be blaming themselves.

They usually end up openly admitting they hardly ever read newspapers and magazines, that when they put on the radio, it's to listen to music, and when they switch on the television, it's to watch their favourite melodrama.

The Meech Lake saga is a good example of this. Everyone claimed that no one knew what the Accord was really about.

And that's true. Even people normally interested in these kinds of things couldn't name Quebec's five conditions.

Yet everyone agreed that they'd heard altogether too much about the Meech Lake Accord.

In reality, people started paying attention to the issue two or three months before the Accord failed. Before that, no one was interested in the least.

Does that mean the media weren't talking about it? Not at all. They talked about nothing but the Accord, which explains the Meech Lake overload. People heard, but they didn't listen. They skimmed the headlines and moved on.

The media, especially newspapers, published thousands of articles about the Accord. Background information, analyses, commentary, editorials from every angle. One paper alone published more than 1,500 articles on the issue in less than a year.

The radio and TV news spent hours discussing Meech Lake.

It was easy to get informed about Meech Lake. But first, you had to want to.

During the 1980 Referendum, the media discussed the issue back and forth over several months. And in general, the media did a remarkable job informing the public about the various issues involved.

But now, they are doing more than simply informing.

Consciously or otherwise, the media almost always put the emphasis on anything and everything that would support the nationalist side. Journalists are making an effort to highlight information and analysis that might move people towards a higher degree of support for Quebec autonomy, leading to independence.

People might not have noticed it, but in almost all the news items dealing with politics, culture, economy, or diplomacy, the media almost always dealt with Canada and Quebec as if they were two separate entities, two different countries. At Cannes, there were films from Canada and Quebec. There was Canadian literature, and Quebec literature. The Quebec economy turned in a better performance than the Canadian economy. Mr. Mulroney pointed to Quebec and Canada as examples. Mr. Bourassa maintained that Quebec had less to lose than Canada. Nelson Mandela was planning to visit Canada and Quebec . . .

We would have never heard such things 20 years ago. The media avoided mentioning Quebec at all. There was Canadian music. The Canadian economy. Canadian films were well represented at Cannes and the Queen of England was on a royal visit to Canada.

There was no conspiracy. Journalists did not get together and agree to use one name and not another, or to emphasize one angle and not another.

Above and beyond the objective information they supply, they themselves had become willing victims of the "favourable juncture."

The idea had wormed its way into every sector of society, including newsrooms and boardrooms. There were no more taboo words, and self-censorship diminished.

That's what I mean when I say that the media accompanied the current situation.

They didn't distort anything. They simply reported, but this time they didn't hold themselves back from joining the parade.

But there's more to it than that.

The media amplify events. That's how their influence, good or bad, goes beyond their function. If *La Presse* runs a statement by an ex-federalist who has swung over to the independence side as its lead, the paper is not being less objective. But it will create an important chain reaction among its readers.

If the *Journal de Montréal* turns its front page over to the latest big nationalist demonstration, the number of participants at the next march will double.

The choice of headlines and the placement of one subject over another are not always innocent. And even when they are, they help the situation move one way or another.

English-Canadian journalists have accused the Quebec media of being too nationalist. They would be if they didn't faithfully reflect the population's state of mind.

In other words, our media are not fomenting revolution. But they could be accused of lacking objectivity if they didn't report on it.

From that point of view, we could say that they did what they had to do and did it well.

By their very nature, by amplifying the effects of the movements and positions they are bound to report on, they contributed to what seems to be a consensus.

They don't create favourable situations. But by talking about them, they can make them more favourable. Or more fragile.

In fact, sometimes it's hard to tell what the real sound is, and how much of what we're hearing is the amplifier.

Whither Meech Lake?

When Mr. Bourassa returned to power in Quebec, after several years in obscurity, he decided to make his mission the salvation of Quebec and Canada. It would be child's play, it seemed, in this time of post-Referendum depression and furious individualism, to concoct a solution that wouldn't offend anyone, and wouldn't awaken the suspicions of the sovereignty movement, which was practically dead in any case.

He went to English Canada and offered to bring Quebec into the Canadian Constitution at the lowest possible price. Ottawa and the English provinces, holding the upper hand since the 1980 Referendum, were in no mood to make concessions to a quarrelsome Quebec.

Besides which, everyone wanted to straighten out the mess once and for all, assured as they were that the monster would not awaken from its slumber.

So, Mr. Bourassa puffed up his narrow chest, pretended to raise his voice, struck the table with his usually timid fist, and proposed the famous five conditions that would constitute the heart of an eventual agreement between the parties.

The time was well chosen. No one in Canada or Quebec cared about the issue. And besides, the content was so meagre that no one could possibly object to it.

Meech Lake? Never heard of it.

The population was surprised to discover that such a place even existed. Or that such an accord did, too.

The 11 premiers had adopted it. The provincial legislatures had three years to approve it. "*Une simple affaire de routine*," they said in French. "Just a rubber stamp," they said in English.

It was in the bag. Mr. Bourassa could go back to his favourite object of contemplation: the economy.

Then the roof fell in.

Once English Canada found out what was going on, they suspected someone was trying to slip a fast one past them. Goddamned Quebec again, trying to get unfair privileges, not leaving anything for anyone else!

Besides, they were a bunch of racists, too. Didn't this Bourassa just bring in Bill 178, which made the English of Quebec the biggest martyrs on the international scene?

We began to witness the most outrageous kind of farce. English-Canadian women sprang to the defence of Quebec women, who needed no such attention. Provinces that had always despised the first nations maintained that they should be part of the agreement.

Bill Vander Zalm stated that there were ten distinct societies in Canada, not just one.

Meanwhile, the *québécois*, calm and serene, watched with bemusement as English Canada, whipped and tortured by a thousand contrary emotions, went through convulsions.

Pierre Elliott Trudeau announced he was going to save Canada once again. Robert Bourassa served notice that his were minimum conditions. Brian Mulroney declared that national reconciliation was close at hand.

Then, the farce turned to tragedy. English Canada turned on Quebec, using the French-speaking minorities as a way of showing its displeasure.

Quebeckers, who up until then could not have cared less, woke up and began defending this scrap of paper whose contents they were totally ignorant of. McKenna, Wells, and Filmon, for a variety of reasons, decided to sabotage the agreement.

People started going off the deep end. Gil Rémillard let loose with thunderous threats, then retreated into hair-splitting tactics designed to reassure.

Mr. Bourassa displayed his usual confidence. But the business class couldn't take it any more. "Sign the Accord, or you'll see what'll happen!"

The tragedy deepened. Things started falling apart.

Lucien Bouchard quit. Conservative MPs followed suit. At the last minute, Brian Mulroney decided to save the day. The day was saved. At a hurriedly called meeting in Ottawa, the first ministers did not say no . . . and almost said yes.

Everyone went home. Only two weeks to deadline. Then one week. Then a few days.

Everybody thought the Savages had been put in their place long ago. But they'd forgotten the last of the

Mohicans who was still hanging around, and who'd gotten himself elected in Manitoba.

He stood up straight in the Legislative Assembly and, with a slash of his tomahawk, chopped the Accord into little bits. Damned Indian!

And that was that. It was all the Indians' fault.

The hypocrites among the Conservatives, Liberals, and NDP rent their garments and went into convulsions of feigned pain. They had done everything in their power to block the agreement and torpedo it using every possible tactic. Now it was all the system's fault: it had allowed one man to grind the process to a halt.

Finally, we had our scapegoat. Use him for all he's worth, then let's get back to important things.

The people of Quebec had taken a very circuitous route. At first, they were totally indifferent to Meech Lake. Then, as English Canadians appeared to want to put it asunder, they began working to keep it joined. As events unfurled, they got the distinct feeling they were being rejected out of hand, and decided collectively that the Accord wasn't worth the paper it was printed on and that, after all, it was probably better for it not to have been adopted.

At first they were furious when their minimum conditions were rejected. But by the time Elijah Harper got around to axing the deal, they applauded. That Indian wasn't so bad after all!

On that dark day, more than one observer declared that Canada was kaput.

Mr. Bourassa stated that Quebec was and would always remain a distinct society, which some people took as a unilateral declaration of independence.

He added that Quebec would never return to the table with the other premiers, but would sign bilateral agreements with Ottawa instead. Which, by the way, it had always done.

What a brave man that Bourassa is!

The timing was perfect: a few days before Saint-Jean-Baptiste Day, June 24. The people of Quebec would finally have a chance to show their feelings.

Which they did, with grandeur and dignity, in the largest parade the nation had ever seen.

By losing Canada, the failure of Meech Lake might have saved Quebec.

At least that's the perception people had and still have in Quebec.

Is that really the truth?

It just might be.

The whole question, the whole infernal, dirty mess, misunderstood, distorted, used for demagogic purposes, painted black or in glowing colours, served up steaming or ice cold, actually revealed the basic essence of the problem, the true historical issue.

All the frustration and hatred built up on both sides for the past 200 years had surfaced, and the eminently artificial nature of Canada was revealed.

The fine words and noble actions had failed. A silly little scrap of paper blew up in our faces and suddenly we gazed upon the bottomless pit before us: the deep divisions that separate us and that have never been more than glossed over to maintain appearances.

René Lévesque would have appreciated this learning experience. He always said we had to negotiate with Ottawa and the provinces, if only to obtain proof that it could never work. Time showed he was right, and now Robert Bourassa would harvest the fruits of this *beau risque.*

Personally, I was afraid to the very end that the Accord would be ratified. Like everyone else, I realized the price people were willing to pay to reach an agreement.

Had it been ratified, we would have probably lapsed into lethargy for a long time to come.

How long? I have no idea. But had the Accord been approved, English Canada would have been furious.

The hatred it would have shown Quebec would have had its effect, and the movement would have picked up again.

The rejection of the agreement certainly accelerated the entire process in a very tangible way.

Rarely have we seen such a murky business lead to such clear results.

We should be grateful.

The whole story is a sordid one, to be sure. I never thought we would have to sink to such depths to reach the heights afterwards. But since it happened that way and it served our interests, we would be foolish not to use it to our advantage, just because we don't like how it fell into our lap.

After all, the present favourable situation might be nothing more than a splendid morning after a sordid night. Who knows?

The International Scene

It's not true that Quebeckers aren't interested in what's happening in the rest of the world. They don't show enough interest for some people's taste, and they might not be able to provide an in-depth analysis of the international scene, but they know what's happening, and what's happening influences them.

They know that the world has undergone some big changes over the past year. They know that the East Bloc countries have thrown off their former totalitarian regimes and, without the threat of Russian tanks, they have tasted the pleasures of national sovereignty.

I say "pleasures" because the advantages, in their case, might not be felt until later. They have to start all over again, unfortunately, and the rebuilding effort must be daunting for them.

But they are sovereign peoples again. Finally, without constant deference to Moscow, they can make decisions that serve their own interests.

The movement that began at the end of the last century is fulfilling its potential: the end of the great empires, the affirmation of national sovereignties, the building of a new internationalism.

There was no internationalism in the time of colonial empires. There was only servitude of one nation by another.

At the time, people believed those empires were eternal. Political observers back then did not reckon on how strong feelings of belonging and emancipation really are.

Little by little, people understood that true internationalism can come only as a result of the recognition of sovereign nations dealing on an equal basis.

Some simplistic minds — Pierre Elliott Trudeau is an example — thought that the creation of larger groups of countries would put an end to national sovereignties. That was simply a way of denying uncomfortable realities that they preferred not to see.

Today, two movements are developing alongside each other, and feeding off each other. Nations are declaring their sovereignty and, above and beyond their differences and particular traits they so jealously safeguard, they are uniting to promote the interests they do share.

Just as national sovereignty does not flower in an atmosphere of autarchy, internationalism cannot have any legitimacy if it is not founded on common acceptance of corresponding national sovereignties.

The twentieth century will go down in history as the era when nationalist movements moved into an internationalist phase.

The recent upheaval in the East Bloc countries should convince even the most sceptical observers.

Throughout the world, people are recognizing the importance of these events. Quebeckers are keeping a watchful eye.

Events are helping us understand that the sovereignty of peoples is not the exception, but the rule.

We've also come to understand that if all peoples find this progression normal, then perhaps Quebec is not an exception in the march of history, and that it can follow this same path.

The more international Quebec becomes, the more it will seek sovereignty. That's exactly what is happening today, and recent events have helped us understand this progression.

A Glance at the Papers

At first glance, they don't seem to have much importance, let alone connection. But the day-to-day events that fill the nooks and crannies of the newspapers can be of great help when it comes to understanding a situation.

They are part of the political juncture; they inform us of its progress.

Over the last year, some unexpected events occurred. Here is a sample.

The Saint-Jean-Baptiste parade: the largest and grandest demonstration in our history, the peaceful will of a people stating its desire to exist.

The Canada Day celebrations: a good many organizations and municipal governments boycott the festivities, including the government of Quebec City. Unthinkable 20 years ago.

Sault Ste. Marie: the spontaneous reaction of thousands of *québécois* to the wave of racism in English Canada. Racism in English Canada has always existed, but its most recent manifestations have created strong reaction, whereas in the past, general indifference greeted them.

"O Canada" booed at Olympic Stadium: never before seen. On three different occasions, the Stadium crowd greeted the national anthem of Canada with lusty boos at Expos games. Normally, sports fans are not inclined to participate in this kind of display. The situation has to have sunk really low before they'll demonstrate this way.

You can tally up these little incidents yourself. Most of them are unprecedented.

Add them to the major elements that create a political situation, and you'll see that the current juncture is different from past events in 1960, 1970, and 1980.

Something really has changed. Though it might be too early to speak of a true consensus building around Quebec sovereignty, it wouldn't be erroneous to say that the movement is a strong and powerful one.

But it isn't irreversible. We have to be able to maintain it.

The stage is set. We should seek inspiration in events and not waste a single minute. It's time for an all-out effort that will lead us to our goal.

Of course. But what do we do now?

PART TWO
What Do We Do Now?

Among supporters of sovereignty, everyone agrees that we have to act fast. Of course. If the situation is as positive as people say it is, then we should seize the moment.

Things change quickly in this world of ours. Nothing guarantees that the fervour of the moment won't soon turn to indifference, or that the exceptional circumstances supporting the movement will continue forever.

Do we have the means for quick action? Do we have the political will to do it? Will we recognize the obstacles that could impede our progress? Do we really know what we want to do, with whom, and how?

What do we do now?

Right or wrong, I have the feeling that, right now, we are deploying our forces on all fronts and having a little trouble concentrating our attention in an efficient way. We are holding all the positions of strength, that's true, but will we have the means to maintain these fortresses long enough?

Personally, I believe we have to simplify our goals, avoid the pitfalls, and assemble our troops as rapidly as possible for the final assault.

That hasn't been done. There is still no end of confusion over the definition of goals. Distinct society? Sovereignty? New constitutional agreements? Sovereignty-association? Associated states? Superstructure?

All these notions, and others still, continue to inhabit the landscape. The consensus that so many people talk about is really a consensus around these propositions as a group, rather than around any single one of them. Prune, cut back, clear the air, choose.

Pitfalls of all kinds will be more frequent in the months to come. We might end up falling into Bourassa's and Mulroney's trap, but we could just as easily fall into one of our own making if we don't clear the ground upon which we are advancing.

To know how to weigh our strengths, distrust alliances, avoid detours and shortcuts, refuse interminable negotiations, and go on the offensive.

For the time being, the fact that our forces are scattered does help our cause. The adversary, harassed from all sides, doesn't know where to expend his energy. But beware, this state of affairs won't last. First, because the adversary will recover his wits — that's inevitable — and secondly, a frontal attack will soon have to take over from harassment.

Recognize our comrades, unite our forces, convince, get organized, obtain international recognition.

I'll be discussing all these issues in the following pages. I'll be giving suggestions. Possible choices. The will to act. And act fast.

The Nation before the Party?

Now that's a fine formulation. *The nation before the party.* No one will be able to challenge it; no one will dare to. The proposition is generous, it appeals to the highest ideals, it speaks of unanimity and creates healthy reflection in the minds of even the fiercest supporters.

The nation seems to be threatened. Therefore, let us set aside our personal opinions and put off the inevitable struggles between political parties.

Invented by Bernard Landry, vice-president of the Parti québécois, the proposition has made its way into people's minds. It soon became something akin to an article of faith.

I wouldn't think twice about adopting it if Washington or Moscow were threatening to flatten Quebec with its nuclear arsenal, or if Clyde Wells were invading Labrador with his army of millions.

Thank God we don't have to face that! And if the nation is threatened, it's on a symbolic level only. The failure of Meech Lake might inspire the creation of new organizations, but they will never lead to a fictitious unanimity from which Robert Bourassa would be the only one to benefit.

Let me explain what I mean.

Let's look at the facts as they are. Let's strip them bare of their media-supplied sugar-coating and the fantasy interpretations that have been made from the few cryptic sentences coaxed out of Robert Bourassa at those times when he preferred to say nothing, which is his usual tactic.

Two major parties share the National Assembly in Quebec City. One of them, the Parti québécois, is for independence, and its primary objective is to make Quebec a sovereign state. The other party, the Liberals, still believes in federalism, as far as I can tell. Despite the failure of Meech Lake, the Liberals continue to seek refuge in a vague wait-and-see attitude, under the fallacious pretext of avoiding the apprehended economic chaos.

Mr. Bourassa came out against "cap-in-hand federalism," but he has continued sharing a bed with Brian Mulroney. And if he happens to get up, it'll only be to travel from one bed to the next. Federalism in a canopy bed (is this what he calls the superstructure?).

The truth is that Mr. Bourassa doesn't know where he's going, any more than his party does, and he's trying to stall for time to avoid any perilous paths that might triumph over his pusillanimity.

I've never doubted that Mr. Bourassa is an honest and sincere man. And he does have the defence of Quebec's interests at heart.

But his sense of those interests is completely different from Mr. Parizeau's idea. The belief that they are pursuing the same objective is a dangerous illusion.

In other words, if we want the nation to reign supreme over the party, we'll first have to make sure that the notion of the nation is the same for everyone and, most of all, that everyone agrees with the degree of sovereignty the nation is meant to achieve.

If not, someone, somewhere, is getting shafted.

In this particular case, Mr. Bourassa is running the show. He's the premier, he makes the decisions. Mr. Parizeau can do all the proposing he wants, but Mr. Bourassa will dispose, according to his rhythm, his manner, his propensities.

We know many things about Mr. Parizeau's nation; we know absolutely nothing about Mr. Bourassa's. That's why it's very dangerous for supporters of sovereignty to be any more generous than necessary. Knowing Mr. Bourassa's diabolical skill, they might very well end up in the cold, just like before, in the not-so-distant future.

I think the day will soon come when Mr. Bourassa will make Quebeckers an offer totally unacceptable to supporters of true sovereignty. From that day on, we will have no choice but to turn to the Parti québécois. That doesn't mean we'll have forgotten the nation. On the contrary. But finally, we will have understood one thing: the only political party whose program offers a sovereign nation is the Parti québécois.

I have always dreamed, and I still dream, of a time when all Quebec political parties will have sovereignty as part of their platform. Were that to happen, we would choose only among party platforms.

But at this point in our history, that dream seems so far removed from reality that I don't dare believe in it.

If that happens, so much the better. But if it doesn't, which seems more likely, the pro-sovereignty forces will have wasted their time on the sidelines. They'll have to reverse their stance and make up for their lost credibility. It will be no small task for them to get the sovereignty movement back on track again.

Mr. Bourassa can make whatever decision he likes. He can choose to wait for the next election, or decide to call a referendum on a question of his choosing. Or he can hesitate and do nothing at all. He can cut the deck the way he likes and choose the time and place for a battle of his design.

I'm not saying Mr. Parizeau shouldn't cooperate with Mr. Bourassa as long as it's possible. Neither am I saying that Parti québécois militants should reject Liberal Party nationalists. I am not advising our political parties to tear each other to bits in public view and lose sight of the common goals that may exist. What I am saying is that unanimous opinion is very rare; only the extremely powerful can call for unanimity without risking their careers and positions.

Besides, I am against unanimous opinion.

For two reasons. First, because those who fancy that unanimity is on their side have no concern or care for the goals and interests of other people. (Have you ever seen anyone triumph unanimously over his or her adversary, then display true generosity afterwards?)

And secondly, because unanimity is often the logical extension of totalitarian regimes.

Unless unanimity is short-term, and used in extreme situations, it is always contrary to democracy.

It drowns dissidence in sloganeering; political paranoia is its only motivation.

I like societies that are not unanimous. I would be perfectly happy if Quebec independence came about through a democratic vote by a simple majority of Quebeckers.

I repeat: the nation before the party, despite the grandeur the slogan inspires, implies dangers so serious that those who wish to use the formulation should discuss it in depth first.

I distrust it, not only on principle, but for tactical reasons.

For the time being, only the Parti québécois supports Quebec sovereignty. For the time being, the nationhood of which I dream is offered by the party for which I work. For the time being, there is no other choice, and I won't make one until the others have shown me their true colours.

Our Goal

There must be one goal only: the sovereignty of Quebec.

If I've said it once, I've said it a thousand times. That's because it's not as clear as it might seem.

For the last 30 years, we've been beating around the bush, hoping one day that some magic inspiration would propel us head-first into the miracle of coherent thought.

We are all acquainted with René Lévesque's states of mind. One step forward, two steps back, rush and retreat, hesitation and hand-wringing, excuses and head-long plunges, from peevishness to inspiration — his personal drama threw the troops and the population as a whole into total confusion.

We are acquainted with all the different proposals that have plotted out the progress of Quebec society and have divided rather than united us. Laurendeau and Dunton, who were able to define the crisis without finding any solution; Pépin and Robarts, who ushered in renewed federalism; Pierre Elliott Trudeau, who offered us a bilingual realm from sea to sea, a vision more philosophical than political; Mulroney and national reconciliation; followed by associated states and sovereignty-association, and a confederation of regions, and the fifty-first American state, and the superstructure, and this and that and everything but the kitchen sink.

And though the notion of sovereignty has progressed all the while, it is still weighed down by all manner of variations, some sincere, others not, but all preventing us from seeing things in clear relief.

I am putting aside those ideas that concern Canada as a whole, and retaining only those that address power for Quebec.

Why? Simply because Jean Chrétien, and Brian Mulroney, and all the other Canadians will forever be our adversaries. I have no advice for them; their fate does not concern me and if they are confused, well then, so be it.

But when confusion overwhelms my side, I am moved and saddened.

You can call my side the nationalists. There are all kinds of them, and I am told they are everywhere, but they do not share a common goal.

Beware of the illusion of legions of well-intentioned people marching in the same direction — are they really? The answer is no.

Let's take the business class. They are nationalists. They are recent but heart-felt converts. Do they support sovereignty as many insist they do? Not at all. They have stated that they're not afraid of independence; they have never come out in favour of it. On the contrary. They will keep on dodging it until the last minute.

Business people have never chosen sovereignty. If ever they accept it, you'll know it's because they have no other choice.

They don't support the same goal the Parti québécois does. Everyone should see that. They might be our temporary allies in the current situation. But we should never draft them into our army and stupidly imagine that they will march to the same drummer into that glorious day.

What about Liberal Party members? A good many of them, so we are told, are nationalists, though they have never chosen sovereignty either. Of course, if their leader led them in that direction, they would probably follow him, but would they follow another leader who would steer them in a different direction? Probably. Some of them might support sovereignty, but most of them are in search of a "less far-reaching" solution.

Independence doesn't frighten them any more either. But that doesn't mean they would be ready to take the plunge — far from it.

What is their goal? It's hard to say. At least for the time being, it would be a terrible mistake to associate them too strongly with the movement towards sovereignty.

The nationalist illusion must not screen reality.

Then there's Mr. Bourassa himself. He's a nationalist, of course, just as everyone else is. But is his goal the same as ours? Not in the least. And until notice to the contrary, his major objective is to keep us from reaching ours.

Of course, of course, you tell me, a good percentage of the electorate would be ready to vote for sovereignty if Mr. Bourassa was proposing it.

But he isn't, and he's not going to.

Instead, he is proposing a superstructure about which we know absolutely nothing. Unfortunately, it's enough to stimulate some naive minds. Oh well, we can always console ourselves, at least he's proposing something, which is better than nothing.

Enough dreaming. If you decipher Mr. Bourassa's vague proposals, you'll see he's offering us the same eternal quibble to win a few powers and a little extra freedom, whereas a different, less taxing fight would bring us more quickly and more surely into full possession of all powers and all the freedom we need.

It's easy to denounce Quebec's enemies. It's a lot more difficult to attack Mr. Bourassa, who has always been and remains a true *québécois*, and who honestly believes that it's not in Quebec's interest to achieve sovereignty.

But we'll have to do just that, because there's no one more efficient than Mr. Bourassa when it comes to putting the brakes on the movement towards sovereignty. He'll let things drag on as we await his conversion. Then he'll offer a solution that seems to contain something new, knowing full well that such a move will be enough to win him the support of most of his party faithful.

He's a nationalist, true. But he doesn't believe in sovereignty.

What about the Conservative MPs from Quebec, currently in the House of Commons — those who haven't quit? They're nationalist, too. Of course. But are they for sovereignty? Let's take a closer look.

First, hats off to them. They've defended Quebec's interests in Ottawa with a great deal of vigour and tenacity. No one can challenge their sincerity. Unlike the Liberal MPs and their leaders, Trudeau and Chrétien, who turned against Quebec, the better to debase it, and who have continued to wallow in their offal, the Conservative MPs have always maintained a dignified position.

That being said, I don't see that their objective is Quebec sovereignty. I am convinced that most of them would come running back to Quebec with a big smile on their face if independence were proclaimed tomorrow.

They're not really against it. But they're not really for it either.

I might be accused of intransigence. I might even be accused of rejecting people whose views are close to ours, and who might one day join our ranks.

It's true: I am intransigent. But that's because I want our goal to be defined with absolute clarity; those who support it must do so with absolute clarity. I don't see why people would follow us down a path that we ourselves don't dare take.

But I'm not rejecting anyone, far from it. I don't care if people are last-minute converts, or if they've been there since Day One. (We'll need plenty more last-minute converts to get over the top.) I ask them to share in our goal as quickly as possible but, in the meantime, I have to conclude that they're moving alongside us, not with us. And parallel lines, no matter how close they are, never meet.

We have to consider such people as objective allies under the circumstances, since they display, day in and day out, the inanity of the Canadian federal system. In that way, they serve a teaching purpose for the Quebec population. That being said, they have yet to state that they want to change it. If they remain inside the government, it's probably because they still hope to change the regime.

There is nothing wrong with their actions. Far from it. But they are still not sovereignty-minded actions.

There is a group of federal MPs who have left their respective parties to form what has been called the Bloc québécois. They were elected to serve in Ottawa, and they continue to occupy their seats in the federal capital. They were not elected as *souverainistes*, but having undergone conversion along the way, they now present themselves as being in favour of sovereignty. Eager to put their decision to the electoral test, they ran a pro-sovereignty candidate in the Montreal riding of Laurier-Sainte-Marie. The candidate won in a sort of mini-referendum which, *a posteriori*, seems to have proved them right.

They say they are for sovereignty, and we have to take their word for it. But Mr. Lucien Bouchard, their leader, is still talking sovereignty-association, and he has stated that René Lévesque is his inspiration. And that worries me.

First, because Mr. Bouchard was one of the first who agreed to run René Lévesque's *beau risque* in Ottawa. It turned out to be a bad risk; it almost killed the Parti québécois and the sovereignty movement with it. And secondly, sovereignty-association is a rather foggy invention devised to make the population believe we can have independence without leaving Canada, and without any unpleasantness for anyone. This demagogic idea hides what's really at stake in a "hyphenless" sovereignty, which the Parti québécois is backing once again.

I regret to inform Mr. Bouchard and those who might follow him in his vision that, if sovereignty-association is their objective, then we are not on the same team.

We're not talking semantics. We're not talking nuances. There is a fundamental difference between the two goals. In one, association with Canada is an essential element of the program. In the other, this association, though desirable, is only an add-on to the fundamental choice that Quebeckers must make between sovereignty and Canadian federalism.

I am speaking of the goal only. Later on, I'll discuss the relevance of pro-sovereignty MPs in Ottawa.

Meanwhile, we will have to tune our instruments to the same key. I can't imagine holding a referendum in which we would offer both sovereignty and sovereignty-association.

Yet we'll have to go into battle together if we intend to win anything at all.

Mr. Bouchard will have to choose: either share our goal and stop talking about sovereignty-association, or else hold onto that outmoded idea, and we'll know we're not at all on the same wavelength. In that case, the Parti québécois, instead of greeting him with open arms, had better exercise extreme caution with him.

I seem to be preaching for the one true church.

Not at all! That's not what I'm saying. People are free to think anything they want to; the truth can be found on all sides, at least part of the truth.

But I also believe this: A political organization cannot offer several fundamentally contradictory goals at the same time.

I repeat: the objective must be absolutely clear. Those men and women who do not believe in it are free to go elsewhere to work for their own goals.

My words are aimed at Parti québécois members and their leaders who might be — and already have been — tempted to trust just about everyone without realizing the dangers of such an attitude. Everyone who believes in sovereignty is a nationalist. But not all nationalists believe in sovereignty.

I'm not judging. People have done very well defending Quebec's interests under a variety of banners. But we have chosen the banner of Quebec sovereignty, and that objective alone will be our rallying point for all our actions.

Then, there is the Youth Wing of the federal Liberal Party that is pulling away from Jean Chrétien and joining the *québécois* "consensus." They supported Gilles Duceppe in the riding of Laurier-Sainte-Marie and worked for his election.

I believe they sincerely share our goals. But they'll have to prove it by joining the ranks of the Parti québécois.

What about the Youth Wing of the provincial Liberals? They want to steer their party towards "wide-ranging autonomy" for Quebec.

They say they're for sovereignty but, when you listen closely to their explanations, you begin to wonder whose side they're on. They talk about an elected supranational government. They talk about sharing currency, defence, external affairs, maybe even transport with Canada.

In my opinion, all that has a strange resemblance to sovereignty-association, though maybe it does go a little further.

The Youth Wing is going to try to push their party in this direction. They have a good chance of succeeding, at least in part. That's not a bad thing. That will move things along. It could go far.

But in the meantime, we can't say for certain whether they share the same goal we do. Especially since their leader, Robert Bourassa, continues his circular trajectory.

And though he has nice things to say about them, he knows he's the one running the show. He's not going to let the party go any further than he wants it to go.

I'm glad to see young people taking up the cause. I only hope they will follow through with their beliefs to the end and reach a position of sovereignty without hyphens.

Let's not forget the talkers and the writers. They come from every corner.

They've done a lot of talking and writing lately.

They have done us a service of sorts. The mere fact that they can discuss sovereignty without denouncing it in hysterical tones helps advance the cause. The mere fact that they don't envision it in the same negative way is grist for our mill. The mere fact that they note its increasing popularity without taking fright makes the prospect seem less dreadful to some sectors of society.

But that's not reason enough to make us believe they share our objective.

When Father Georges-Henri Lévesque confessed he was beginning to consider sovereignty after having fought it most of his life, I'd love to believe him, but when he starts fantasizing about the future of a Canada divided into four or five regions, I can't quite figure out his true intentions. When a stubborn man like Lévesque vaguely admits that he might change his mind, then we know opinion in Quebec is undergoing a profound overhaul in the right direction. But it would be naive to conclude too hastily that public opinion has been wholly seduced by the charms of sovereignty.

No end of intellectuals have taken pen in hand to devise elaborate scenarios designed to guide our future action. They give out their advice to anyone willing to listen, enjoying their role as oracles in a political situation that they did not foresee and that destroys the relevance of the very scenarios they are offering.

Léon Dion, for example, has always hesitated, just as André Laurendeau did in the past, afraid to draw the conclusions that should follow his brilliant analyses. Today, Dion seems a little less circumspect, and he has flirted with mixed results with "the idea"; perhaps he has even made his bed and is willing to lie in it. But for Dion and others like him, the real choice has yet to be made. Actually, he is only following the practice of certain intellectuals who would like to be right *a posteriori,* having set up the framework for the correct hypotheses, and who would like to pass themselves off as leaders of public opinion. Dion goes whichever way the wind blows, justifying his capriciousness with an appeal to the pretext of exact science.

That's just fine with me if the influence of these intellectuals helps swell the ranks of the pro-sovereignty side. But if their fervour is a passing fancy, I won't be destroyed.

Personally, I have always considered them a little dangerous. Maybe it's because they want to come across as original thinkers, or maybe it's their habit of scholarly hair-splitting. But they always seem to break everything into shades of meaning, or drown the issue in rhetorical precaution, or engage in counting angels on the head of a pin in order not to discredit the profession.

It is not always easy to know what they really mean. Clarity is not their strong point, and defining goals is a strange practice for them. They prefer interminable discussions presented at heavily subsidized colloquia, safe from the movement on the street which might frazzle their finely tuned minds.

They have an important role to play and I'm not trying to take it away from them. We should open our ears to the often enlightening discussions they have about our goals, but watch out! If we pay too much attention to them, we might find ourselves drifting off course. Which we must not do.

Next come the big union organizations that have recently taken a stand in total favour of sovereignty. We can't say the same for their members.

There seems to be no room for doubt in their case: sovereignty and nothing but. This is cause for rejoicing, since union people, with the exception of the metal workers, were hardly the first to join the fight. I remember being nearly lynched — I'm exaggerating, of course — during a CNTU convention. The delegates were so fiercely against separation that I was glad to get out of there alive.

Now they've joined our side. Far be it from me to play the wet blanket.

Let's not forget all those people who, after the failure of the Meech Lake Accord, suddenly swung around and joined the side they had only recently been fighting.

They are the ones saying, "Since they don't want us, we'll go it alone."

I met quite a few people like that who, after voting No on the 1980 Referendum, swore they wouldn't be fooled again. They promised that if ever another referendum was called, they'd know which way to choose.

Their conversion is sincere and moving. But as soon as you talk sovereignty to them, they start hesitating. Yes, but ... Maybe, if we really don't have the choice ... Is Quebec really strong enough economically?

These recent converts know what they don't want. But they're not so sure they know what they do want. They've come a long way, but for them, sovereignty is often a last resort.

They're fragile converts. They can easily go the other way. They're still a little afraid, and unacquainted with our goal. All the more reason to present one that's as clear as possible, in a straightforward way, without word games, and without trying to sweeten the pill.

Sovereignty is difficult to gain. It's even more difficult to internalize. Everyone should be aware of this from the start. In the fall of 1990, the idea was wrapped in an atmosphere of euphoria, which was a pleasure to see. Though that atmosphere is encouraging, it shouldn't lead us into an artificial paradise of head-long flight or abusive simplification.

I've talked about a lot of different people, and I'm sure I've forgotten some. The prospect is exciting, and I know any number of old and not-so-old believers who are starting to hope and dream again just like in the good old days.

And now, their sons and daughters, apparently so docile and resigned such a short time ago, are pushing them into involvement and urging them to take up the fight.

Never before, in the last 30 years, has the goal seemed so close.

Yet I'm convinced that a lot of people are still beating around the bush. They're afraid to take the plunge. It's dangerous to think that all alliances are possible now, and that nothing can stop us in our quest for sovereignty.

Nothing is irreversible. We should say it once and say it again. There are no end of pitfalls that might open up under our feet. That's why the Parti québécois must remain as determined as it is now, and make its foremost goal — Quebec sovereignty — the rallying point of the majority of Quebeckers, and not simply one discussion point among many, or one item among many at the negotiating table, or one bargaining chip among nationalists of all colours.

Our goal is not negotiable. Neither at parliamentary commissions, nor at constitutional assemblies, nor in discussions at estates-general, nor behind closed doors, nor out in the open.

Constitutional bickering can distract us. The nationalist reawakening can delude us. Let's keep a cool head and do what's necessary to rally as many people as possible to our goal: the sovereignty of Quebec.

Weighing Our Strengths

In the past, the pro-sovereignty side has so often fallen into illusion that it might not be a bad idea to examine the situation closely with a view to avoiding the errors of the past.

I remember when many supporters of independence stated with a straight face that Trudeau was a separatist, and that his program was nothing more than a way of leading Quebec into sovereignty. A laughable proposition, but it had a demoralizing effect on the troops, who turned to imaginary allies in the midst of battles lost before they had begun.

Today, Robert Bourassa is playing the same role. And we are in danger of falling into the same trap.

I still remember René Lévesque (my obsession) who naively believed that, after a victory by the Yes side,

English Canada would cease all resistance and bend in good grace to the will of Quebec. Mr. Lévesque believed, despite all that history taught, in the democratic sense of English Canadians. He had to face the brutal facts the day they sold him down the river.

I still remember the 1980 Referendum, when the pro-sovereignty side vastly underestimated the federalists' strength, as well as their contempt for the democratic rules set up by the Quebec government.

What's the state of things now?

Viewed in the general euphoria of the moment, everyone seems to be our ally, and no one our enemy.

Jean Chrétien? He's finished.

Brian Mulroney? Deep down, he's on our side.

The NDP? They've already come out in favour of Quebec's right to self-determination.

Clyde Wells, Newfoundland's premier? He doesn't have the influence.

The RCMP and the army? They wouldn't dare — they'd be too afraid of the international community's disapproval.

The Americans? They're not for, but they're not against either.

The North American multinationals? They know Quebec favours free trade.

The Canadian union movement? They wouldn't dare cross the Quebec unions.

Robert Bourassa? He's the one who will end up leading us to independence.

And so forth and so on, *ad infinitum.*

All our adversaries are down for the count, and all reasonable people are on our side. The opportunists, inspired by the polls, will jump on the bandwagon as fast as their legs can carry them.

Euphoria is a fine sensation. But so dangerous as to ruin all our prospects.

Let's be realistic!

We are still surrounded by powerful adversaries who won't hesitate to use all the means at their disposal to block sovereignty.

Opinion polls have revealed that a good percentage of English Canada is ready to let Quebec go if such is Quebeckers' desire. In some corners, this scenario is even viewed as a positive development.

But remember, if people say that's what they think, it's only because they don't believe it will ever occur. The day the impossible happens, the day Quebec chooses sovereignty, we'll see an unprecedented uproar in English Canada. The great majority of English Canadians believes in Canada and sees Quebec separation as something repugnant. It's one thing to answer an opinion poll survey when the threat isn't real; it's another thing to face Quebec's firm resolve to leave Confederation.

Wait and see. There will be threats, demands that the RCMP and the army intervene, talk of an economic blockade; accusations of treason will ring out, international pressures will be brought to bear, garments will be rent and lamentations heard. In other words, everything possible will be done to halt sovereignty.

That won't keep us from moving forward. If we remain firm in our resolve, nothing will be able to stop us.

But we should realize right now that considerable forces will be marshalled against us, and that we should be prepared to face them. We should make an effort to prepare ourselves psychologically, instead of wasting time in idle conversation in our comfortable salons.

Remember Jean Chrétien? He can still hurt us.

People say he's finished, that he's powerless. That's not true. He is still the most popular political figure in English Canada. Even in Quebec, he can count on support which, though not considerable, is still to be reckoned with. We know he's a man without principles, that he'll stop at nothing. We know that, as far as he's concerned, the end justifies the means. We know he's used to strong-arm tactics, and that he's never been afraid to spit on Quebec to preserve his chances in Canada. We also know that Old Man Trudeau is still waiting in the wings, that he's still dangerous. The two of them might not be as powerful as in 1980, but when things get hot, don't be surprised to see them again.

Brian Mulroney is still prime minister of Canada as far as I know. Unless he resigns, which is not very likely, he will hold the job for the next two years.

Though he's a Quebecker and his sympathy for Quebec's aspirations is real, he's not about to sit back and watch as Canada is wrenched apart.

Neither Mulroney nor any other Canadian prime minister who may come after him will accept a declaration of independence from Quebec without putting up a fierce fight. Is he down in the polls? Is he currently the most unpopular prime minister in Canadian history? So what! He's still the elected head of the government and he has enormous means at his disposal to use as he wishes. I'm not saying he's going to order the RCMP and the army to our border; I'm saying he can do it if he wants to and that we should keep that fact in mind. And I'm willing to bet that the day he begins fulminating against Quebec — and that has already begun — putting himself forward as Canada's saviour, his popularity will rise at a spectacular rate.

He will be sorely tempted to do just that, since it may be his only way of saving his skin. Beware of those adversaries who appear weak; they are the most dangerous.

What would you say to a coalition of Conservatives, Liberals, and the NDP together in a government of national union whose mission is to save Canada?

A fantasy? I'd like to think so, too. But I ask you to think hard about it, as I've done.

What about the Americans?

We shouldn't distrust them on principle; they're no worse than anyone else. It is our *duty* to distrust them.

We have the strategic duty to distrust everyone who, for one reason or another, might attempt to move against us and might have the means to do it. The Americans are among such people.

So much the better if they continue to maintain their present neutrality. If that keeps up, we won't need any special strategy, and won't need to take their strength into account. But, since we know they are unpredictable, we have the duty to act as if . . . as if they were not in agreement and might decide to show their unhappiness.

It's better to consider that possibility than pretend the Americans simply don't exist or, worse, as some people have done, imagine they will support Quebec sovereignty, the better to control Canada.

What about Robert Bourassa? I've said it once and I'll say it again: Robert Bourassa is not for sovereignty and we would be mistaken if we believed he could ever be our ally. In the next few months, I wouldn't be surprised if he proposed something that resembled sovereignty just a little, just enough to sow seeds of confusion in the minds of the population. He has started showing his true colours, and already the most naive among us are hurrying to fall into his trap.

Bourassa is a setter of traps. If we fall into one, Quebec sovereignty will be a thing of the past.

Other forces could come into play against us. We should prepare ourselves to face them. And we shouldn't forget the effect of circumstances beyond our control.

The Oka Crisis should have taught us how a minor incident can quickly degenerate into a major crisis and disrupt the timetable, change the political landscape, divide the population.

All manner of unexpected events can occur, which might considerably weaken our momentum. Events are unpredictable by their nature. Still, we can prepare ourselves to a certain extent against the unexpected by realizing that it might, and probably will, occur.

The most serious mistake we could make now would be to overestimate our own strengths and underestimate the adversary.

We are in a good position. We can win. But we will win only if we distinguish between our true allies and our real enemies, and if we give the latter all the attention it takes to control them.

I don't want to be a wet blanket. On the contrary, I'm feeling optimistic these days. But I do want to instill a little realism into the debate.

International Relations

The pro-sovereignty side didn't wait for the approval of the business class to start talking about internationalism. We've always known it and we've always said it. No one can ignore the fact: Quebec can't step onto the international stage until it's declared its independence.

Only sovereign states can take part in major international organizations and maintain equal relations with other sovereign states.

At the present time, Quebec is only a province of Canada. Ottawa, and Ottawa alone, has the power to conduct international relations and define the country's foreign policy.

Quebec has been able to maintain a few pretences in the past. It had to fight like the dickens to be recognized in Dakar, Algiers, and Paris, and we all know what the results were. Interminable quarrels with Ottawa and a kind of

Platonic recognition designed to satisfy us provincials, but with no real importance or weight on the international scene.

Because Quebec is only a province among others, and because we have never experienced political sovereignty, we often have difficulty situating ourselves in relation to the rest of the world. We have never made any attempt to define an international policy that bears our own stamp.

We're rank amateurs in this area. No use pretending. If we were called upon to develop foreign policy tomorrow, we would be in very bad shape.

Whom should we deal with and what should the main lines of our policy be? Which are the governments that would be most inclined to recognize a sovereign Quebec, and how far are they willing to go to support us? What international treaties should we sign first? Who are the adversaries who would seek to destabilize us? What means do we have to begin negotiations, and on what points? Who's who in the world? Who manipulates; who is manipulated? What markets can we safeguard, and what ones can we conquer? To whom can we open our doors; whom should we keep out? Will we play the neutrality game or line up with one alliance or another? Will we side with Israel or the Palestinians, and at what cost?

These are but a few sample questions. Unfortunately, in most cases, we have no answer.

Yet we're going to have to come up with answers in the near future.

Up until now, we've been able to toy with the idea, to play with concepts, give our personal opinion on one subject or another, laugh over the awkwardness of the

Americans or rejoice over the developments in the Soviet Union.

Sovereignty seemed so distant that no one saw the need to project ourselves onto the international stage.

But in the current state of things, it would be irresponsible of us not to immediately take the necessary measures to prepare for such an eventuality.

It's up to the Parti québécois to do it. It's the party which, once in power, will have to assume Quebec's international responsibilities.

I believe it should start doing that now, as if Quebec already was a sovereign state.

Not only would the Parti define a true international policy for itself, it would do so in an area that Robert Bourassa wants no part of, because he is and wishes to remain the premier of a Canadian province. Besides, it will upset Ottawa.

Mr. Bourassa doesn't have the power to make pronouncements about the situation in South Africa. That's up to Mr. Mulroney to do. But as leader of the Opposition and eventual head of a sovereign state, Mr. Parizeau can very well set down the policies of the government he will eventually form.

Policy is no matter for improvisation, of course. That's why the Parti québécois must immediately set down the main lines of a sovereign Quebec's foreign policy.

The seeds of this policy already exist in the Parti's platform. But now's the time to start going further.

It's all the more pressing because, in the months to come, all around the world people will be wondering

·about the orientations of our foreign policy. The firmness of our intentions will be put to the test.

Though we are unaccustomed to playing the big game on the international scene, we can still count on a number of specialists, here in Quebec and elsewhere, who can be called upon in confidence to put their knowledge to work for us.

We have no interest in taking other states by surprise. Don't forget we will have to convince them of the legitimacy of a sovereign Quebec and facilitate our entry into major international organizations. Other nations will be glad to assist us if they know of our intentions ahead of time.

This being said, even if they are aware of our intentions, some countries will not find it in their interest to recognize us. Russia, for example, which has a problem with the aspirations towards sovereignty of a number of its republics, might drag its feet, hoping to block the pro-sovereignty forces within its own borders.

As well, no one should take it for granted that the United States will be the first to support us, despite their apparent neutrality and the fact that they no longer reject our aspirations out of hand.

What about Canada? Seeing the fateful moment draw nearer, Canada will do all within its power to stop the movement. Throughout the world, it will undermine our efforts, wherever we make them.

In the past, we were full of illusions. I remember that René Lévesque displayed dreadful naivety in this area.

It's fine to hope for the best. But we'd be better off acting as though things were going to be extremely tough, and build our scenarios from that position.

Which means that, starting now, we should begin working on those men and women who hold positions of power in the world. We must establish contacts, forge links, inform, discuss, even negotiate agreements that, though secret, will help us determine whom we can count on.

For starters, Mr. Parizeau should travel more. He is less recognized abroad than Mr. Lévesque was, or even Mr. Bourassa. We have to solve this problem without delay.

He should send emissaries wherever it serves our interest to do so.

We have already made contacts in various places around the world. A good number of *québécois* have created bonds based on professional activities and friendship with people in power beyond our borders.

We should discreetly call upon them. I'm thinking of Louise Beaudoin, Claude Morin, Louis Bernard, the former Quebec delegates abroad; I'm thinking of the former ministers of the Lévesque government who have travelled widely and might be made to resume their service.

There's no use counting on Mr. Bourassa to do this work. It would be easier if he were interested, of course, since he could have it done at the government's expense, whereas we have to depend on our own personal means. Though meagre, a part of them should be used to this end.

I'm not talking about playing Errol Flynn, or tilting at windmills, or raising our flag in foreign capitals. Neither am I talking about offering free vacations in the sun to a few upper-level Parti workers who fancy themselves as ambassador to Rio or Rome.

I'm talking about doing the down-to-earth, thankless, but essential job of breaking out of our isolation on the international scene, and seeking out the recognition of other countries on the big stage.

These emissaries must not set out empty-handed and empty-headed. We're asking for something; we'll have to have something to offer. Our homework has to be well done, and our research must show those with whom we wish to negotiate that we have interests in common.

We'll have to know just who it is we're speaking to. Some of our so-called partners will excuse themselves for diplomatic reasons, others for ideological motives. Who will our real partners be, and which ones should we speak to first?

Who can give us the most, and to whom can we offer the most? Who will be in power five years from now, and who will have been toppled? Who, in the shadows, has the most influence, and who, currently in the limelight, is no more than a façade?

In other words, let's do what everyone else does on the international scene.

This being said, some people will probably consider me a sort of sorcerer's apprentice in a low-class patriotic side-show. Others might interpret these actions as the agitations of a parallel government or a government-in-exile.

Nothing of the sort. To be taken seriously, we'll have to do our work in a serious manner. That means not wasting energy, and starting now to prepare the ground on which, tomorrow, come what may, we'll have to fight for our place in the sun.

Because, whether we think about it or not, or prefer to put the prospect aside, Canada will also be there on the international scene.

Association or not, a sovereign Quebec will have to aim for Canada's recognition, and work to make the break in the best conditions possible.

That's why it's imperative, right now, to imagine the new situation that will be created between our two countries, and the accommodations that might be made on both sides in order to serve the interests of the two parties.

Let me give an example. A sovereign Quebec would separate Canada into two distinct parts: the Maritime provinces on one side, Ontario and the West on the other. In a difficult situation, this geographic position could provide Quebec with a certain bargaining power. But since we want to avoid difficult situations, we should consider the necessary arrangements to keep Canada from being inconvenienced by this drawback.

Contrary to what many people think, there should be no drawbacks involved. Consider Alaska, which is more than 1,000 kilometres from the continental United States, separated by Canada. This separation does not create any major problems because Canada and the United States agreed upon the necessary rights of passage to keep the two parts together.

Canada and Quebec could come to a similar agreement. I believe that Quebec, in a stronger position in this regard, should make an immediate proposal on rights of passage to Canada. Not that we should expect it to be accepted — no responsible Canadian could accept that eventuality — but at least it will be heard, and in the process neutralize those demagogues who hold up the prospect of the Pakistanization of Canada to frighten the population.

The same goes for sharing Canadian assets and debts. Why not start talking about it right away? Why not make a certain number of proposals that express Quebec's interests, thereby launching a discussion that will obviously have to be continued at the negotiating table?

It's not easy to picture Canada as a foreign country. But we have to if we want to imagine an independent Quebec. You can't have one without the other.

Neither is it easy to picture Quebec taking a seat at the United Nations, or naming an ambassador to Tokyo. But we'll have to make our imaginations work if we want to convince ourselves that we can go all the way.

Again, I remember René Lévesque. Once, a little facetiously, someone introduced him as the future president of the future republic of Quebec. He grimaced, as only he knew how to. It wasn't out of modesty. Deep down, he didn't believe it. One day I told him that if he didn't believe in it, he'd have a hard time convincing other people.

We have to believe in a sovereign Quebec. Now's the time to start behaving like a sovereign state on the international scene.

That doesn't mean Mr. Parizeau should pretend he's the president of the republic; it means explaining what the policies of this president will be, and the policies of his government and his people.

That doesn't mean playing at Quebec sovereignty; it means displaying our determination to carry it through, and to do so with the utmost gravity.

That doesn't mean just preparing the world, but preparing ourselves to take our place in a competent way on the international scene.

That means getting ready to elect, not the premier of the province of Quebec, but the president of the republic of Quebec.

An Emergency Plan

We can imagine two scenarios leading to Quebec sovereignty (I'm putting aside the *coup d'état*, a method that never interested anybody).

1. The Quebec government will negotiate a number of points leading to separation from Ottawa, and the two parties will agree upon a date for a declaration of independence.

2. The Quebec government will unilaterally declare sovereignty, and from this *fait accompli*, negotiations will eventually take place with Ottawa.

In the first case, no major problems arise. If everything occurs as expected, the transfer of powers and responsibilities will be done in an orderly fashion and according to a timetable, leaving both parties time to get adjusted to the new reality.

However, it may be that discussions will not go as smoothly as we'd like. Unexpected complications may destroy the entire process. Worse, Ottawa may simply refuse to negotiate, forcing Quebec to act unilaterally.

It may also happen that Quebec, for strategic reasons, will unilaterally declare sovereignty. If that's the case, we should be prepared to face the music.

Now is the time to begin developing an emergency plan by which the Quebec government can remain master of the situation, no matter the circumstances.

Since it is highly improbable that Robert Bourassa will unilaterally declare Quebec independence, if the break should occur in that fashion, we can assume that a Parti québécois government will be the one to take that responsibility.

It is up to the Parti québécois to foresee this kind of situation, and seek immediate solutions to the problems that might occur.

Obviously, this kind of emergency plan cannot be discussed during the PQ annual meeting. If it's not secret, it must at least be restricted to a few.

I have no intention of offering solutions here; other people are more competent than I am in that area. Instead, I will put forward a number of questions that should be answered in the plan.

1. From one day to the next, how might Quebec exercise all the powers of a sovereign state and assume all responsibilities?

2. How can public administration be entirely concentrated in Quebec City, and how can income and sales tax be collected without difficulty?

3. Who will look after public security? The police, of course. But we can also imagine that military personnel might want to offer their services to Quebec. Who will command them? How much time will it take before they are ready? (I don't believe this issue has ever been discussed among sovereignty supporters. To my knowledge, no serious contact has been made with *québécois* members of the military who might be willing to serve a sovereign Quebec. These contacts can only be made secretly, I realize. But they must be made. Is this an alarmist or fantasy scenario? I don't think so. Only the normal procedure for any sovereign nation.)

4. How can the population be kept constantly informed of its government's decisions and the attitude it would be preferable to take in a given circumstance? Should the state "draft" the news media for a period of time? (I can already hear accusations of dictatorship, propaganda and enslavement of the media. I'm not naive enough not to see the danger of this tack, but neither am I naive enough not to think it necessary in certain circumstances.)

5. Will citizens of Quebec, under the circumstances, be able to continue using their Canadian passports, or should a sovereign Quebec act with the utmost speed to issue its own passports?

6. Will Quebec delegations abroad be elevated to the status of embassies from one day to the next? How can they be made to be recognized as such, and how can we replace the personnel who, for one reason or another, may want to resign?

7. How can the government of Quebec head off any interruptions in old-age pension cheques, unemployment

insurance, or other social benefits that, up until now, have been administered in Ottawa?

8. Will we close our borders or leave them open?

9. What should we do with the St. Lawrence Seaway?

10. How might Ottawa reply to a unilateral declaration; what means will it choose? What is our short-term bargaining position?

11. How, from one day to the next, can those federal bureaucrats who wish it be transferred to Quebec and immediately integrated into the Quebec civil service?

12. How can we win public support during this difficult enterprise?

I've put forward a mere 12 questions, whereas there will be questions by the hundreds for the government. And that government will have to find the solutions in the shortest time possible.

Is it too much to ask of those who would govern us in a sovereign nation to try to bring forward solutions to these problems, and do so now?

Is it too much to ask them to begin developing solutions that will keep us from falling into chaos and allow us to reach our goal with as little conflict as possible?

Is it too much to ask them to plan rather than patch together solutions for a situation that might turn out to be difficult?

I know that by putting forward these kinds of questions, I might find myself accused of needlessly frightening the population, or of conjuring up unrealistic scenarios that no one, in any case, wants to consider.

To those who might accuse me of this, let me answer that a nation is reassured when its leaders consider all the hypotheses, and prepare to face situations with the necessary sense of responsibility, instead of simply waving the flag and promising an imaginary paradise that will inevitably be of short duration.

My answer is that you need a good organization to get to paradise.

My answer is that people are less frightened when they're well prepared, and that they have more courage when they know ahead of time what's at stake.

My answer is that improvisation leads necessarily to authoritarianism, whereas proper preparation can help us preserve democracy, even in the most difficult circumstances.

I have nothing against wasting time in parliamentary commissions and scouring the countryside in search of votes. But I also want to do what's necessary so that the move into sovereignty will be as harmonious as possible.

Sovereignty can be a happy event, or a disappointment. A lot depends on the way we accede to it.

The Bélanger-Campeau Commission

First there was talk of an estates-general. Now we're having the Bélanger-Campeau Commission . . . an enlarged commission, if you please!

Why? Don't ask me!

Individuals and groups have come parading before the Commission and, for the hundredth time, repeating everything they have always said.

Did we expect to see Jean Chrétien and his gang come cap in hand and make declarations in favour of Quebec sovereignty?

Did we expect to hear the CNTU and the FTQ justify the War Measures Act and beg Pierre Trudeau to return?

Did we expect the ecology freaks to appear to demand clear-cutting of forests in an independent Quebec?

Did we expect the Warriors to come and lay down their

arms before an astounded assembly, and offer Robert Bourassa a scarf so he could hide his face?

Or perhaps we were hoping that Clyde Wells would show up and, in homage to Quebec, hand over the keys to Labrador.

Of course, nothing of the sort happened. Day after day, we have been listening to the same old speeches, with the usual varying degrees of subtlety and research, from the same old voices.

Nothing more, nothing less.

At the end of which, the Commissioners will write a long report that, in theory, will attempt to describe the main lines of a "consensus."

In the current state of affairs, the conclusion can either be: "Quebec should attain sovereignty," or "Quebec should not attain sovereignty." Then will come a variety of considerations on how to do it.

In the first case, Mr. Bourassa will gather his supporters together in a convention and ask them to go along with what he wants, and forget about the Commission's recommendations.

In the second case, Mr. Parizeau will have to retreat back to his base and continue his action where he last left it, and urge his troops to continue the noble fight for sovereignty.

In other words, we will have wasted several months, and we still won't be any wiser about the real intentions of the Quebec people.

But, for the time being, we don't have the choice. The Commission is up and running and part of the political landscape. And since it's part of the landscape, we might as well use it.

For the pro-sovereignty side, using it means turning it into a podium to clarify positions, present timetables, raise the stakes.

Since the Commission and its work are attracting and will continue to attract a great deal of media attention, the population will have its ears open wider than usual.

The time will be right to transmit the pro-sovereignty message and make sure that, when voting day comes, a good majority of Quebeckers will vote YES for independence.

We'll have to increase the number of large and small public meetings. We'll have to speak from podiums in every part and parcel of Quebec.

We'll have to reinforce the structures and organization of the Parti québécois and speed up recruiting.

We'll have to launch the referendum or electoral campaign immediately.

There won't be a better time to do it.

Meanwhile, we'll have to keep pushing Mr. Bourassa into taking a position. Force him into a corner and demand that he seek the people's mandate as quickly as possible.

If the Bélanger-Campeau Commission is to have any usefulness, it must be able to recommend to the government a strategy that will make the people of Quebec part of the action as soon as possible.

Because that's what's at stake, that and nothing more.

We've done enough talking.

I'll repeat myself again: putting off the deadline may prove fatal to us. An unexpected occurrence is always possible. Serious, unpredictable events can throw us into mortal chaos.

The Bélanger-Campeau Commission? Sure, it's part of the landscape. But we should act as though it was already dead and buried.

Ontabec or Quetario?

A new idea made the rounds last year. An alliance between Quebec and Ontario. We're back in 1841, and the union of Upper and Lower Canada.

What an invention! When all is said and done, Canada means so little to us that we could get along quite well without it, if it weren't for Ontario. Think about it: $30 billion of trade every year!

We could even invent a brand-new name for this country. Choose one yourself: Quetario or Ontabec?

The bedfellowship of David Peterson and Robert Bourassa inspired this kind of talk. Though David Peterson is no longer leader of Ontario, the idea is still around.

It's true that Ontario and Quebec have a lot of interests in common, and it's been that way for a long time. Whether Quebec is independent or not, that won't change. Afterwards, as it was before, trade between the two partners will continue to be important, and Ontario's French-speaking minority, about the same in number as Quebec's English minority, will want to see relations remain as close as possible.

But this kind of sovereignty-association idea is no better than the one that was defeated in 1980. We can't decide to be associated with anyone until we have determined our own future ourselves, and this is as true now as it was 11 years ago. I have nothing against an association with Ontario. But to take this association and transform it into an idea for a new country is simply a way of diverting the attention of the *québécois* people away from the essential decision they have to make. This decision is so serious that all other projects, far-fetched or not, should be put aside so the basic proposal can be better examined.

Deep down, this idea was created to hide our fear of independence. Anything but independence.

In the months ahead, all sorts of proposals will rise to the surface; all will be designed to make us believe there is an alternative to Quebec sovereignty. Many people will fall into these traps, and we'll waste precious time trying to reveal them for what they are.

Quetario or Ontabec, it all adds up to the same business: pure garbage.

Since we've sunk so low, why not keep it up, just for fun?

New-Quebec or Quebrunswick, that has a ring to it!

Alberbec or Queberta is even better.

Manitobec is music to my ears. Quenitoba swings, too.

I've got just the deal! Let's start a chain of taco restaurants. What do we call it?

Mexbec! What else?

The Bloc Québécois

Sometimes history plays ironic games with us.

There has always been disagreement within the independence movement. Should we or shouldn't we send MPs to Ottawa?

The Rassemblement pour l'Indépendence Nationale and the Parti québécois always said no. But they were never able to convince all their members to give up on the idea. At different times, some of them decided to take the plunge. The results were not very conclusive.

And now, suddenly, without any conspiracy, strategy, or major campaign, we find ourselves with a "Bloc québécois" in Ottawa, about a dozen different MPs. It's no use asking whether it's a good or bad thing. They're there, and we'll have to act accordingly.

What does it all mean?

So far, these MPs, except for Gilles Duceppe, represent only themselves. They are directed by one man, Lucien Bouchard, who answers only to himself.

These men say they support sovereignty and we have to take their word for it. I don't think we should doubt their sincerity or honesty.

But it's worthwhile asking ourselves what they're doing in Ottawa, and just how effective their work can be.

. And also what they'll do when the time comes to pull out of Ottawa and repatriate their forces to Quebec.

Let's take Lucien Bouchard. He has set himself up as the leader of the troops without firing a shot, and no one seems ready to challenge him. That's fine. But he doesn't belong to any party — the Bloc québécois not being a party — and it's hard to know what his intentions are.

He speaks *urbi et orbi* of unanimity and unity, but if I understand correctly, this unity is supposed to revolve around his person. He has never spoken of joining the Parti québécois. He claims to be above and outside political parties. He flirts as easily with Robert Bourassa as with Jacques Parizeau — maybe more easily with the former than the latter.

He seems to think everyone is moving in the same direction, which is his, and he presents himself, if I'm not mistaken, as the man who will eventually lead the vital forces of the nation.

He doesn't put it that way. But that's the impression he gives.

He has even gone as far as launching a fund-raising campaign whose sole objective is to raise money to help him spread the good news all across our fair land.

That's just fine. So far, he hasn't done anything to harm the cause. On the contrary.

But that state of affairs won't last much longer. Sooner or later, he'll have to win a democratic mandate if he wants to present himself as the legitimate representative of his cause.

For the time being, he's playing the outsider. I have nothing against outsiders — I'm one myself.

But outsiders should hold no ambitions. They represent only themselves, cannot claim to speak in the name of anyone else. The role they play is limited, and they must stick to it, or risk being accused of plotting behind the backs of the legitimate leaders, without the drawbacks of the democratic process.

Some people already picture Mr. Bouchard in Mr. Parizeau's job. That's fine with me, but if those are his intentions, he'll first have to become a member of the Parti québécois and challenge the leadership of its current president according to the time-honoured processes.

Mr. Bouchard isn't saying anything, and that bothers me. He never mentions the Parti québécois, and to my knowledge, he has never recognized Mr. Parizeau's priority as leader of the pro-sovereignty movement.

His self-appointed outsider's role is hardly reassuring for anybody. In my opinion, in the very near future, he should publicly join the foot-soldiers of the movement, instead of presenting himself as the grand leader-in-waiting of the republic.

The sovereignty movement could certainly use a man of Mr. Bouchard's qualities, and his ministerial experience in Ottawa only adds to his competence. But he'll have to disperse the cloud of doubt surrounding his true intentions, and humbly accept that he must put in his time in the movement, like everybody else.

Let's be frank. He's playing the messiah a little bit too much for my taste, and I don't believe in this particular messiah any more than in all the others.

I know we need leaders. But we don't need those so-called saviours who have a way of showing up at all the crucial points in our history.

That being said, he remains the non-elected leader of the Bloc québécois, and we must accept him as such.

Georges Matthews, in his most recent book entitled *L'accord*, foresaw a situation wherein a certain number of federal MPs would sit as independents in favour of sovereignty in Ottawa.

He considered this a favourable development, and thought they should remain in Ottawa as long as necessary to move things along.

I agree with Georges Matthews.

Although it is a condition of mine that they be in solidarity with the Parti québécois and coordinate their actions with those of the party, I still believe they can be more useful in the federal capital, for a certain length of time, than in the pro-sovereignty wave in Quebec.

There are not many of them, but we can expect their number to swell in the coming months. Already, some MPs, especially Conservatives, have gone so far that they might soon take the plunge. It's good for them to have a place to land; the Bloc québécois can take them in comfortably . . . in the interim.

But just what will they do . . . in the interim?

First, they can be our eyes and ears. They are in a good position to know what is going on in Parliament and, besides, they can make use of their contacts in government to gather valuable information.

They can keep an eye on what other parliamentarians are doing, including those in the Opposition. They can attack them if the need arises, in the Commons and in public.

They can scrutinize bills that are put forward and the disposition of the public purse to make sure Quebec is receiving its fair share. (Yes, Quebec is still part of Confederation. Yes, we pay taxes of all kinds to Ottawa and, yes, we have the right to be served fairly.)

They do have a place in Ottawa. They are like the Trojan horse behind enemy lines.

They can also cause disruption. It's not a very glorious role, it won't necessarily win you showers of praise, but it can be useful. While big events are taking place in Quebec, it wouldn't be a bad thing to have someone throwing up smokescreens in the adversary's camp.

I'll grant them enough imagination and skill to use all the tricks in the book to slow down the parliamentary machine if they judge it necessary. There aren't many of them? That doesn't matter! We saw what a single member of a provincial parliament could do when he decided to torpedo the Meech Lake Accord. The parliamentary game, when you want to deal in bad faith (don't be afraid to call it that, because that's what it is), is full of hidden procedural treasures.

They will be spat upon and cursed, but that's what they expect.

They can perform an educational function by sabotaging the system from within to reveal its inequity.

Canadian federalism is rotten to the core. Its function has been reduced, for all intents and purposes, to serving Ontario's interests alone. It would be relatively easy for these MPs to prove this.

They can make contacts with English-Canadian MPs to explain our intentions and objectives, and make them see that Quebec sovereignty can also serve English-Canadian interests.

They can play the same role with foreign visitors and journalists who will surely want to meet them to have their point of view explained.

In short, they will have their hands full. Besides the jobs I have listed, they'll add on their own as the need arises.

But . . . in the interim, there is another more important task for them: working for the unity of the Quebec sovereignty movement. There's no time to lose. Soon they will be returning to Quebec — how could they solicit another mandate as federal MPs? — to join, in one function or another, the only political structure that can fulfill their pro-sovereignty feelings: the Parti québécois.

It wouldn't be a bad thing if they thought about it now.

Then again, they could always do something else. Such as transplanting the Bloc québécois to the Quebec political arena, or continuing to preach action outside and above existing parties, or calling upon Liberals and PQ supporters to join a new party that they will proceed to invent. But if they did this, they would be making a very serious mistake.

I know what it's like, I've experienced the break-up of the pro-sovereignty side. I did everything I could to bring together our forces within the Parti québécois, despite the fears many of us had.

To carry out effective action, you must have solidarity among all the forces.

I believe that's more important now than ever. I am urging all forces to join together within the Parti québécois, for I believe this party, pro-sovereignty once again under Jacques Parizeau's leadership, represents the heart of the movement, and that the PQ is its most solid organization.

No one should forget this. No one should claim it would be painless to start all over again, at square one, with no risks involved.

If the Bloc québécois MPs are realistic, they will agree with me and see there is no other solution.

The battle will be hard. We can't afford to scatter our forces. We are willing to grant that the Bloc québécois has a job to do in Ottawa . . . in the interim. But it would be intolerable, once the moment has come, for them not to dissolve into the greater pro-sovereignty whole.

Let's remember that the decisive battle will take place in Quebec City. And that the declaration of independence will come from nowhere else but there.

The French-speaking Minorities

We know that French-speaking populations living in the English provinces fear Quebec's accession to sovereignty. Though they are sympathetic to Quebec's cause, they believe that a separate Quebec would have no more influence on Canada; their situation, already fragile, would deteriorate even further.

It's important for the pro-sovereignty side — notably, the Parti québécois — to quickly calm their fears by developing a firm policy regarding them. A stand by the PQ would presumably help them look upon the future with less apprehension.

We must first remember, and remind them, that English Canada has always mistreated them, no matter what degree of power Quebec has had over its history.

On one hand, people have said that when Quebec was weak, the French-speaking minorities suffered because

English Canada was under no pressure, and could conveniently ignore them.

But it's also been said that when Quebec was strong, and even threatened to pull out of Confederation, that state of affairs created problems for the French-speaking minorities; they fell victim to an English backlash. In other words, they were hostages to English Canada, objects of revenge for poor relations with Quebec.

The two theses are in contradiction. Unfortunately, they are both accurate. In essence, English Canada has always striven to assimilate its French-speaking minorities, and to a great extent it has succeeded, while using language designed to frighten them, whatever the circumstances.

Quebec independence won't be responsible for the death of Canada's French-speaking minorities. It's Confederation, in its workings up to now, that has destroyed them.

Let's be honest. Quebec sovereignty is not going to save the country's French minorities. Some of them are so small and so weak that they have little chance of survival, whatever Quebec's status.

Other of these minority groups — I'm thinking of those in Ontario and New Brunswick — will still have to fight hard and often losing battles. But I think they're strong enough to successfully resist Anglo-Saxon racism that unfortunately surrounds them.

A sovereign Quebec won't make miracles. But it can do something, and now is the time to say what we intend to do.

First, let's assume that the French outside Quebec will want to maintain themselves and, consequently, they will call upon Quebec to support them. Let's not cast doubt on their determination.

Quebec will have to assume its responsibilities. In my opinion, there are two ways.

First, to help consolidate the position of French-speaking populations outside Quebec by signing reciprocal treaties with Canada.

While we're thinking about Canada's French-speaking minorities, let's not forget about the English minority in Quebec. The English in Quebec, despite their incessant complaining, are in an enviable position when you compare them to minorities in other parts of the world.

That should continue. But a sovereign Quebec must demand from Ottawa, by treaty, that its French minorities will receive the same treatment.

That means equivalent institutions, similar rights regarding schools, communication networks of the same order, the same degree of services, etc.

We are not talking about reducing the rights and privileges of Quebec's English minority. We simply want French-speaking populations outside Quebec to enjoy what the English have here.

Canada, and not the provinces, should assume total responsibility in this area.

Canada should take measures so that its Constitution will allow it to act in this way. It should do whatever is necessary to make its recalcitrant provinces see the light.

This action will help Quebec extricate itself from the trap it is now in. On the one hand, Quebec would like to help the French-speaking population in Manitoba, for example, but it can't get involved in other provinces' business without the other provinces getting involved in its business. On the other hand, since Quebec is not dealing on an equal footing with Ottawa, the pressure it can exert on the federal government is so weak, even at the best of times, that the results are scarcely felt.

As I said, we shouldn't expect miracles. The French populations outside Quebec will have to continue struggling to maintain and reinforce their position. However, negotiations between sovereign states will give Quebec much greater weight in this area, and its role will be much more important than it is under the current regime.

Besides, it would certainly be in the interest of the *québécois* and of the French-speaking minorities in Canada if relations between the two communities were maintained and even heightened by increased exchanges.

It's conceivable that a certain percentage of the French-speaking population outside Quebec, discouraged or simply realistic, might decide it's not worth the fight, and that only two choices remain: assimilation, pure and simple, or exile.

Many people have come to that decision over the years. Some have assimilated; others have sought exile in Quebec.

Assimilation will continue to a certain degree. Quebec, sovereign or not, won't be able to do much about it.

We should be moved when people choose exile in Quebec. We should pay more attention to them. Instead, we have done nothing.

I know of entire families who have left Winnipeg or Saskatoon to start life over again in Quebec. They faced a great number of problems, and we didn't lift a finger to help them. Despite that, they survived and integrated into our society.

When it comes time to develop immigration policy, we should give priority to members of the French communities outside Quebec who want to come and join us.

Easy to integrate, determined to remain French, these "immigrants" will make a great contribution to the maintenance of our positions.

With them, it should be said, we'll be winners on every front.

That's why we should establish programs to help them join us in the best possible conditions. That would include paying their travel and relocation costs, offering living costs for a period of time, helping them find jobs and giving them Quebec citizenship, with all the rights and responsibilities that implies, the first day they arrive.

I am not suggesting a policy aimed at depriving the French minorities of their vitality. I am merely offering a way to save those people who have run out of hope of escaping assimilation in the region they now live in and, in the process, help Quebec consolidate the position of its own French majority.

Will they stream into Quebec by the thousands? I doubt it. Exile is as painful for them as it is for others. Yet I do believe that, considering how many have already come in the difficult atmosphere they now face, many more will arrive if we offer them a priority position.

Time is of the essence. The sovereignty forces must begin contacting the French communities outside Quebec and describing the policies they intend to implement in their regard.

Perhaps they will be less apprehensive about their future; perhaps they will even support us in our undertaking.

The English in Quebec

"Our English" are here to stay. A few more thousand may leave, but the majority, I believe, will remain in Quebec, whatever the decisions we make in the months and years to come.

If the situation continues to evolve in its present positive way, that is, towards sovereignty, the English will have to face the facts and take on an identity as Quebeckers. In fact, we are not asking any more of them than we ask of ourselves. When you think about it, it's only been recently, and after more than 400 years of history, that the majority of French-speaking people in Quebec have learned to define themselves as *québécois*.

It's normal for the English to take a little more time to reach the same point. The undertaking is difficult and demands a painful choice: abandoning their identification with the Canadian majority and the immense English-speaking North American community, and accepting minority status in a largely French-speaking Quebec.

A good number of them have already taken this step, but many have still not resigned themselves to it.

They might hesitate less if we made them some real promises. It seems to me that the pro-sovereignty side, despite its openness in the matter, has not paid enough attention to the issue.

The Parti québécois should make a solemn declaration of Quebec's unequivocal will to recognize the historical existence of the English minority, confirming its rights, and guaranteeing it its institutions, language, and freedom of expression.

That doesn't mean promising them a bilingual Quebec. On the contrary. They know and we know that a sovereign Quebec would be more French than it is now. What we're guaranteeing them is this: once the rights of the French majority have been respected in their entirety, there will still be room for them, limited, certainly, but nevertheless real, in which they will be able to live and grow in their own language and culture.

I've always found it petty to force bilingualism on them in their own institutions. I'll say it again: either we accept them, or we reject them. If we accept them, we should go all the way and stop demanding that Dawson College also be called le Collège Dawson, and that the Montreal General Hospital also be known as the Hôpital général de Montréal. We can request them to make the necessary efforts to serve their French-speaking clientele in French within their institutions, but they must have the right to preserve them in their status as English-language institutions.

A majority that has confidence in itself, and that enjoys all the powers of a sovereign state, will certainly run no risk by being generous towards its historical minority.

To act in any other way seems to me unacceptable on every level.

That's why I am asking the Parti québécois to add this solemn declaration to its party platform. Once and for all, let's recognize the rights of the English-speaking minority in an independent Quebec.

I don't think such a declaration would inspire the English to rush out and join the PQ. But I do believe it might reassure them and help them decide to take on a *québécois* identity, and find within themselves the will to build a democratic, generous Quebec alongside us.

Indian Summer

In 1990, Indian summer was hotter than usual. But it left relations between whites and the first nations in the deep-freeze.

It's time to repair the damage, and do it quickly.

Who did the damage? We all did. The whites blinded themselves with self-inflicted guilt, while the aboriginal people shucked off all guilt by putting all the blame on their invaders.

In both cases, we lost all sense of reality. We'll have to get it back if we ever intend to solve the issue once and for all.

It will take time to settle the serious problems that arose from the crisis. The gap is now alarmingly deep between the first nations and the whites. Above and beyond the responsibilities of each of the parties in the shameful confrontations at Oka and elsewhere, we'll need to bind the wounds and recover our senses in order to live together once again. That won't be easy. It'll take will and generosity and no small measure of courage. However, unless the situation degenerates again, time should begin to heal the wounds, and we have good reason to be hopeful.

But if we don't want things to degenerate, we'll have to attack the heart of the problem, now, and not wait for the convalescence to be complete.

Despite the crisis, polls show that a majority of Quebeckers are sympathetic towards the demands of the first nations. Concomitantly, most members of the first nations don't feel any visceral hatred towards us; they're more inclined to seek peaceful solutions with us.

Everyone agrees that Quebec has always treated the first inhabitants of its territory better than the rest of Canada in its respective provinces. That's good, but it's not enough. We'll have to go beyond generosity and begin a process of reason and justice.

Generosity, like charity, is never enough. It's simply a way of forgetting; it tends to perpetuate the injustice that gave rise to it in the first place. Justice is the key. It leaves nothing to chance and does not depend on individual action — no matter how well motivated — to improve society and the fate of all its members.

We can't go on acting as though dispensing varying degrees of generosity to "our Indians" is enough. They're sick of our charity. Instead, we have to show them we can be just.

Where do we start?

As in so many other things, we have to start by getting rid of the federal government. If Quebec had been sovereign during the Oka Crisis, it would have been able to settle the issue more quickly and with less damage. Not because we're better than anyone else, not because we discover solutions when everyone else comes to a dead end, but simply because it's always easier for a single government to determine its objectives and negotiate with another party to reach a solution.

At the present time, the federal government is still in the picture. We don't always have the power to initiate wide-ranging negotiations with the first nations to reach an all-encompassing solution.

The aboriginal peoples "belong" to Ottawa. When the chips are down, Ottawa always decides.

That's why, in this case as in all other cases, we should behave as if Quebec were already a sovereign state.

Mr. Bourassa can't do it. He doesn't want to.

As usual, it's up to the Parti québécois to define a sovereign Quebec's policies in this area, and to immediately begin discussions with the first nations and, if possible, reach an agreement that would become valid the day that independence is declared.

Since the Parti québécois does not form the government, it obviously cannot offer formal guarantees. But it can use this strategy to show the first nations that they're an integral part of the new Quebec, which they can join as free and equal partners.

We have often criticized them for not getting along among themselves, and not knowing what they want. That might be true up to a certain point, but the same could be said for us. The action I'm proposing might very well inspire them to undertake similar actions, which in turn will help them define their objectives and grasp their reality, as we ourselves are striving to do.

I'm very big on the notion of reality, which seems to have escaped both parties.

Among whites, we too often imagine the life of the Indians on their reservations as idyllic, lazy, and parasitic. Since some don't pay taxes, we've decided that none of them does. We think they receive all manner of grants, but that a good number of them live off welfare and spend all day latched onto a bottle, that they accept only those laws that benefit them and reject the others that don't further their cause. Essentially, we see no reason for their perpetual recriminations.

The reality is something else again.

They aren't happy because they're not free. It's as simple as that. True, they are dependent on us, but that's exactly what they find intolerable. Sure, some of them don't pay sales or income tax, but they want to be able to pay their taxes to their own institutions as a way of financing the services they need. All right, they do cost us a lot of money, but that's because, on their narrow band of territory, they don't have the means to develop the economic structures and activities that would free them from need.

That's the reality in 1991. Open your eyes and see. They want to be free, independent, and sovereign. Does that remind you of someone you know?

On their side, they, too, have abandoned all sense of reality, especially when they start calling upon ancestral rights that take them back to a bygone era, denying contemporary history in the process.

They have a habit of forgetting that a lot of things have happened in the last 300 years, and that now, in North America, there are 250 million non-aboriginal people who are here to stay.

Some aboriginal people are like those ecology freaks who want to defend every animal and plant on earth against human beings, as if we weren't part of the system, too. The prophets of the first nations do the same; they're ready to defend their blood brothers and sisters, excluding all the other members of the population in the process.

They're not paying any attention to reality.

This is reality in Quebec. On our territory, there are 58,000 members of the first nations and 6,800,000 "immigrants." No one has been here for 10,000 years. We've all been here for 20, 40, 60 or, at the most, 100 years. Our ancestors don't have to worry about living together; we, the living, do.

No matter how the territory was conquered, the sons of the conquerors will never agree to being pushed into the sea. The aboriginal people will have to live with them, whether they like it or not.

The reality is that the first nations comprise 1/117th of the Quebec population. They may have inalienable rights, but the majority thinks it has a right to some of the territory, too.

The reality is that their traditions, no matter how fine they are, are no better than ours. Sometimes, they can really get in the way.

For example, it used to be in our traditions to "kill the Savages." Should we continue the practice today, in the name of tradition?

To respect a tradition is not to imprison it in folklore. It means making it come alive by adapting it to your own life, not just your ancestors' lives.

Hunting and fishing? For most members of the first

nations, they have ceased to be a reality. For most, they are leisure-time occupations, as they are for whites.

Subsistence? My eye! A small number of Indians still live off hunting and fishing; a small number of whites do as well. The rest of them exist on fast food, the way we do. The expansion of Indian territories is not going to change those habits. Will they go back to spear-fishing and hunting with a bow and arrow the way their ancestors did before we arrived on the scene? Will they spurn the snowmobile, a machine foreign to their ancestral traditions? Will they turn up their noses any more than we have at airplanes and luxury cars?

The reality is that life has changed for the first nations, as it has for us. We should recognize that fact. If we don't, we'll lapse into self-parody by trying to rebuild the world around something that no longer exists.

The reality is that James Bay electricity heats our houses and lights our lights, for whites and Indians alike. If someone decides to blow up the transmission towers, Indians and whites alike will be plunged into darkness, and no one will be able to claim the ancestral light.

Their spiritual chiefs? No better and no worse than ours. No more trustworthy nor infallible nor superstitious than ours. And no less, either.

The protection of the flora and fauna? A recent invention, for Indians and whites alike. It's pure demagoguery to maintain that Indians respected and still respect nature. You see, 1,000 years ago, no one needed to protect it because we were neither numerous nor skilful enough to destroy it. Nature always came out on top, even when people practised the scorched-earth policy.

Consensus? It's a great thing in a village setting, in peacetime. But it doesn't work in a complex, highly populated society, especially in a conflict situation.

All customs and all traditions are not of equal value. Some should be strongly criticized, no matter what nation they belong to.

I have nothing against the traditional Indian way of negotiating, according to which you go back home before sundown — or before rush hour hits the expressways. But whites have their own method of negotiating, and sometimes it gives good results. You have to choose the lesser of two evils.

Let's get back to reality and rebuild the world from 1991 onward.

For the last 300 years, we have been bogged down in petty detail, in a legal labyrinth we might never escape if we keep up this way.

We have to get the cause of the first nations out of the white courts and begin negotiating on a new basis.

If you ask me, it's completely useless to try to research whether the King of France gave such-and-such a piece of land to the Mohawks or the Sulpicians, or to discover in the archives a scrap of paper proving that the aboriginal peoples occupied New York before the Dutch.

I'm not saying that digging through the archives is an uninteresting activity. But that kind of research doesn't get us anywhere, or if it does, it moves things along so slowly that we'll all be dead before the slightest detail gets resolved.

Should the Acadians take back all of Nova Scotia because they occupied it before the British conquerors?

In principle, maybe. But that has nothing to do with reality.

I'm not saying we should start everything over again at square one. We should start exactly where we are now, taking into account our current needs, possibilities, and constraints.

"Treat them as factions and they will act as factions. Treat them as nations and they will act as nations."

Lord Durham said that about the French Canadians more than 150 years ago.

His words should have rung a bell.

In 1985, the Quebec National Assembly recognized as distinct the ten first nations living in the territory of Quebec.

Now, that's reality. All negotiations should begin from that point, and it should be made clear to everyone that no derogation from that principle will be tolerated.

Let's put aside the federal government; so far, they have refused to take this step. Let's begin discussions with our own first nations in hopes that the results obtained will satisfy all parties and be an example and inspiration to the rest of the continent.

As a corollary to the first principle, we will need to add that the ten first nations have the right to self-determination, like any other nation in the world, and that they have the right to exercise sovereignty over the territories that belong to them.

That's where negotiations should begin. Not from what once was, 1,000 years ago, but from this point onward.

Question: Will the first nations decide to create ten distinct countries within Quebec territory, ten countries with an average population of 6,000 each? Would the whites accept such a proposal? Would this proposal, if it's insisted upon, be viable? If not, what degree of autonomy would these territories enjoy? Would it be possible or desirable to join the ten nations in a federation to which a certain number of powers would be granted, and which would constitute the supreme government of the first nations?

Question: What territories are we talking about? "Ancestral" territories — which would make up more than 85 percent of Quebec — or territories on which 58,000 people could live and develop normally into the twenty-first century?

The questions are not idle ones. If we stay stuck in our historical imagination, the negotiations will be doomed before they begin. But if we recover our sense of reality, all accommodations are possible.

Question: Should we establish borders and customs offices along the edges of our respective territories, or should we sign free trade agreements at the outset? Don't all first nations' territories throughout the three Americas comprise a single territory without reference to "white" borders drawn by the different countries? How can we deal with this?

Question: What are the accords and treaties we might wish to sign?

Question: Who negotiates for whom, and with what mandate?

Question: What might be the grounding for a real sociopolitical contract between whites and the first nations?

Question: Are we willing to live in peace and friendship with one another, and under what conditions?

Question: Are we ready to negotiate as one nation to another?

We already know the answer to the last question. The National Assembly, by recognizing Quebec's ten aboriginal nations in 1985, gave its formal consent.

There are no doubt other relevant questions that could be added to this list. The answers can be found in discussions between equal partners.

Recognizing reality is not enough; we also have to recognize the demands it makes on us. In this particular case, the demands are pressing, and we have to move quickly and solve this problem with all due dispatch.

Whites don't need an Indian guerilla war any more than the first nations need a white power structure they hate and that keeps them from taking their destiny in hand.

But we both badly need mutual respect.

Let's say it openly, and say it loud. A sovereign Quebec is ready to negotiate right now, on an equal-nation basis, with the ten first nations living on Quebec soil. The goal: bringing them towards autonomy according to a method of their choosing.

P.S.: You'll notice I did not use the word *native* to speak of members of the first nations. That's because I've always believed the word created confusion, and that they are no more native than I am.

The Majority

French-speaking Quebeckers make up more than 82 percent of Quebec's population. This percentage will most likely increase over the years.

First, we restated the need to protect minority rights. Then we described our intention to return sovereignty to Quebec's first nations. Now the time has come to talk about the rights of Quebec's French-speaking majority.

In our pluralistic societies, we too often forget that majorities do exist, and that they have the right to exist without suffering what I call the dictatorship of the minorities.

The homosexual minority has rights. But they must not be exercised to the detriment of the rights of the heterosexual majority.

The English minority has rights. But they must not be

exercised to the detriment of the rights of the French majority.

Criminals have rights . . .

Blacks have rights . . .

The unemployed have rights . . .

Drug addicts have rights . . .

Moslems have rights . . .

Immigrants and refugees have rights . . .

Cyclists have rights . . .

Don't get me wrong. I don't want to cut back on minority rights in any way. I just want people to remember that majorities do exist and, from time to time, they should enter into consideration.

If one man's freedom ends where another's begins, we could also say that minority rights end when they trample on the majority.

It's pure demagoguery to make people believe that, in the name of pluralism, majorities must submit to every wish the minorities express.

It's pure demagoguery to make Quebeckers of Greek origin believe that their language should have the same status as French.

Just as it's pure demagoguery to try to make people believe that majorities are always in the wrong, that they practise virulent racism, that they get their kicks crushing their minorities as a way of solidifying their power.

Unfortunately, that's true all too often. But it's not true in all cases, and I wish people would start making a few distinctions.

Quebec's French majority has made its mistakes, and we shouldn't hesitate to criticize when the occasion calls for blame. But the majority is not all evil, and from time to time I wish people would admit to its proverbial generosity and tolerance.

In other words, I wish people would listen to something other than the highly amplified vociferations of minority media of all stripes, and hear the voice of the guilt-ridden majority that hardly dares to show its face in public any more.

Yes, I do fear the power of majorities. They tend to dominate rather than tolerate. But I also fear the dictatorship of the minorities, who preach the ascendancy of the small group over the large.

That's all I have to say.

I would just like to remind my readers that the respect of minority rights occurs only when majorities respect themselves.

Referendum or Election?

When all the speeches are made and all the arguments put forward, when all the parties have indulged in their fair share of constitutional fantasies and whims, when we have wasted enough time, we'll have to turn to the people and ask them what they want.

Their mandate should be elicited as quickly as possible but, unfortunately, I'm afraid Mr. Bourassa will decide to drag his feet again and put off the process until the end of his term, in about three years.

If that happens, and I hope I'm wrong, we just might miss our rendezvous with history.

That's why public opinion should be marshalled to force Mr. Bourassa to hold a referendum or election as soon as possible — in 12 or 18 months.

Mr. Bourassa won't do this unless he's subjected to strong and continual pressure from all quarters, all organized groups, every tendency and vital force this nation has. Notably, from the official Opposition, represented by the Parti québécois.

It won't be easy to make him bend. But we'll have to try by all means possible.

It's my opinion that the vast majority of Quebeckers are ready to make up their minds on the question, as long as it's clearly put.

My first choice runs towards a referendum rather than an election, for obvious reasons. First, and most importantly, a referendum lets the people choose a single option, independently of the individuals, parties, platforms, or those often unsavoury deals that underpin an election.

If the *québécois* people, by way of a referendum, choose a sovereign Quebec, they will be asking all parties to rally to the idea and join together to declare independence. If they choose the contrary, as they did in 1980, they will be forbidding all parties to take this road, though they cannot keep certain of them from continuing to promote the idea.

A referendum is not a sure-fire method to prevent confusion in the minds of the electorate. Some people will be for sovereignty as long as it's Mr. Bourassa who is proclaiming it. Others won't want it unless Mr. Parizeau leads them there, and still others will opt for an independent Quebec without its current leaders. But a referendum is a way of reducing confusion to a minimum since, in the voting booth and the privacy of their conscience, voters will be facing but a single question, the answer to which can only be categorical.

It's either YES or NO. The only way they can say "maybe" is by abstaining.

A referendum has an advantage over an election insofar as there is less room for contradictory interpretations according to the particular interest. (As long as the question is clearly put, of course.)

If the Parti québécois is elected, people can always say that the voters didn't really choose sovereignty; they only wanted to display their unhappiness with the Bourassa government. If the Liberals are elected, observers can claim that, though people basically support sovereignty, they fear a sovereign Quebec with Mr. Parizeau at the helm. And so forth and so on. Every possible interpretation will be allowed, which will more often than not serve the interests of Quebec's fiercest opponents.

Besides, in Western democracies, it's very rare to see any party win more than 50 percent of the vote. Our adversaries will point to this and claim that since a minority voted in the government, there is no clear choice for either option.

This can never be the case with a referendum. It's well nigh impossible for the two options to come in neck-and-neck, with the same number of votes.

A majority, no matter how small, cannot fail to emerge as a result of the process.

Obviously, the losers will howl if the majority is narrow. They will claim that 60 percent of the vote constitutes a real victory, or two-thirds, or 80 percent, or whatever. But that won't change the fact that they lost and the others won according to predetermined rules.

No one can deny the victory of one side over the other. The majority decision will have to be respected.

A referendum sets the stage for a clear question, which is far from being the case in an election.

That is, if we want to ask a clear question. That's not always the case, as we saw in 1980. Mr. Bourassa might be tempted to repeat the exploit and offer the electorate a choice among several options, or between two plans, one of which would be completely pro-sovereignty, the other somewhat in the direction of sovereignty.

That's a trap we have to watch for. A question like that should be met with a boycott by the Parti québécois and all the citizenry.

A referendum that takes place in good faith should ask the question clearly, whereas in an election, all sorts of other elements are involved.

In this particular case, everyone wants to know whether Quebeckers want a sovereign Quebec. No more strategies, no more tactics, no more beating around the bush! Now's the time to get moving, and a referendum is the best way to do that.

I repeat: we need a referendum as soon as possible. We have to give the *québécois* people the power to make up their minds on the issue.

Enough estates-generals and constitutional renewal and endless word-mongering.

The Bélanger-Campeau Commission is enough as it is. I don't see what an estates-general could bring to the issue. As for a Quebec constitution, there will be time enough to draft one once the population has decided, even if it means adopting it afterwards.

Why waste time writing the constitution of a sovereign Quebec if the voters decide to stay in Confederation? (Which doesn't mean people can't work on the project.)

First let's find out what we want. There will be time enough later to put a container around the contents.

Mr. Bourassa is telling us more about the frame than the picture. But the picture is what really counts.

I have absolutely no influence on Mr. Bourassa. As I said before, it will be no easy task to convince him to call an early referendum. Still, we must put pressure on him to move in that direction.

If that should fail, we'll have to settle for an election. But, election or referendum, we want it as soon as possible.

Even Mr. Bourassa should concur. For despite his propensity to stall, he knows very well that, if he prolongs the uncertainty surrounding Quebec's future, he may well compromise his pet obsession, which is what he calls economic security.

An election has none of the virtues of a referendum, as I have said. But, if there is no referendum, we'll have to settle for our second choice.

In that case, the Parti québécois will have to be absolutely clear and firm and state, *urbi et orbi*, that if it wins the election, it will take that victory as a mandate for the new Quebec government to declare sovereignty, after negotiations with Ottawa if possible, or unilaterally if necessary.

The Parti will have to dismiss the objections of those who will try to deny the legitimacy of its course of action.

We are still working under a parliamentary system. The party that wins the election has not only the right but the duty to carry out what it was elected to do.

We must make no concessions on our objective. And we must avoid the belief according to which, since the Liberals and the PQ are offering more or less the same thing, voting for one side or the other will make no difference to the real outcome.

It doesn't matter whether you're nationalist or not. It matters whether you're for sovereignty.

What about the Youth Wing of the Liberal Party, which is proposing a kind of sovereignty-association dressed up for the new decade? "I have understood you," Bourassa told them, just as General de Gaulle told the French in Algeria.

He has understood them perfectly well. He has judged them to be positive, realistic, and intriguing.

But I swear to you that he'll do exactly what he wants.

Referendum or election, there are still two sides fighting it out. There's no use trying to convince ourselves or anyone else that everyone, all together, will march happily off to Quebec City, singing, arm in arm, along Highway 20.

Because some people will be taking the other shore of the St. Lawrence. And I don't think there's a bridge strong enough to span the two sides.

Let me sum up my position. A referendum as soon as possible, with a clear question. If not, an election as soon as possible, and let's finally give the people of Quebec a chance to choose their future.

The Question

If you're going to have a referendum, you have to have a question.

We all know just what kind of controversy Mr. Lévesque's question set off in 1980. After a long, explanatory preamble, it avoided querying people directly as to what they wanted. Its only goal, in essence, was to bring Mr. Lévesque comfort by asking the citizenry to approve his choice of strategies.

The question was long and complicated. Later, we saw that it contained a major problem that rendered it completely fallacious.

If you responded with a NO, your answer was interpreted as a rejection of Quebec independence. On the other hand, if you answered with a YES, you were not really coming out in favour of Quebec independence. At the most, you were approving a negotiation process whose objective was far from clear.

Not only does this type of question tend to create confusion in people's minds, it lets everyone interpret the answer to his liking, according to the personal interests at stake.

Which is obviously what would have happened had the YES side won a majority.

Of course, if you're a political leader who can't seem to stop fence-sitting, it's tempting to play both sides at once, and seek an equivocal mandate that will allow you to go on hesitating as long as possible, while swearing to high heaven that you are simply serving democracy.

But when it comes to the future of a people, and you're asking them to make a difficult choice with extremely serious consequences, you can't afford to remain in the domain of vague approximation. You need a clear answer to a clear question, so that endless interpretations won't be possible.

In the months to come, all manner of committees will be convened to write up the question. I'm willing to bet that most of these questions will be tortuous and confused, and designed not to offer Quebeckers a real choice. As in 1980, people will try to construct a question to which, in theory, the voters can only answer YES, but to which, in practice, they would like to answer NO.

That's why, before all these questions start popping up, I've decided to put mine forward. I believe it offers no haven for ambiguity. It is clear, obvious, and leaves no room for interpretation.

I'm not taking credit as its inventor. It's very similar to the one General de Gaulle put to the Algerians during the referendum on independence at the beginning of the 1960s.

It has two parts:

1
DO YOU WANT QUEBEC TO BECOME A SOVEREIGN COUNTRY?
2
DO YOU WANT A SOVEREIGN QUEBEC, INSOFAR AS IT IS POSSIBLE, TO BE ASSOCIATED ECONOMICALLY WITH CANADA?

Voilà. There's no possible way out.

The first part asks the voter to make his or her essential choice. The second part is purely subsidiary to the first, designed only to measure the degree of preference to be given to Canada in economic matters. (To tell the truth, I wouldn't mind at all if the second part disappeared entirely. In my opinion, it's obvious that we'll be associated economically with Canada, as with many other countries. But let's keep it for the time being, since it reflects a historical situation that is deeply ingrained in the collective unconscious.)

The two important words are country and sovereign.

We can hem and haw about the real meaning of the two words, but I think they mean the same thing for most people. But just so there won't be any confusion about definitions, we can use the meanings supplied by, for example, the *Random House Dictionary*:

"Country: the territory of a nation."

"Sovereignty: supreme and independent power or authority in government as possessed or claimed by a state or community."

There's no clearer definition than that. And no room to propagate confusion between *sovereignty* and *independence*, since independence is an integral part of sovereignty.

The dictionary definition should leave no doubt in anyone's mind. I am using it as a way of avoiding the inevitable plethora of definitions, concepts, and prejudices.

Not only is the dictionary definition clear, but it is historically and sociologically accurate.

Now that we understand the question — at least I hope we do — we can move on to the answer.

Voters can answer YES or NO to the first part of the question. Their response will be the expression of their will for or against Quebec sovereignty.

Their answer to the second part of the question is less important, as I said earlier. It expresses a desire that may or may not be feasible.

As in the past, we would not be proposing an economic association with Canada just to have it rejected out of hand. This second part is simply a way of letting Quebeckers tell their leaders the way they would like to see negotiations go with Canada. The answer, positive or negative, does not preclude other associations. It simply takes note of a historical reality, and adds a personal expression to it.

I added the phrase "insofar as it is possible." I believe it is an important qualifier, for it allows us to refuse to follow a course that might turn out to be dangerous for us.

Of course, any association must be made in the interests of all partners. Since it is not written in stone that economic association with Canada is necessarily in everyone's interest, and since the form such an association would take is far from being a subject of absolute agreement, we should be cautious and give our decision makers plenty of flexibility.

In other words, if it's in our interest, that's fine. If not, we'll look elsewhere.

Which is why I say that the answer to the first question is essential. The answer to the second is incidental.

What are the possible answers?

Voters can choose YES or NO on the two parts. There is no equivocation possible.

But voters can answer NO to the first part and YES to the second. What would that imply? It's easy to see: the voter says NO to Quebec sovereignty, but since no one can be sure of the results, in case the majority chooses the YES side on the first part, the voter can express his or her wish that a sovereign Quebec be economically associated with Canada. (In other words, coming out against Quebec sovereignty but, "if things take a turn for the worse," at least try to control the damage.)

That is the question.

I believe the people of Quebec are ready to answer it, which is why I would like them to have that opportunity as soon as possible.

In the meantime, perhaps we should put it to Mr. Bourassa.

We already know how Mr. Parizeau and the Parti québécois would answer.

I'm afraid we'll have to wait a long time for Mr. Bourassa's response. And when it finally comes in, I'm willing to bet it will be NO.

For a very simple reason. The premier of the province of Quebec doesn't think he has what it takes to be the prime minister of a sovereign state.

And he's right.

Now

The very subject of this book forced me to write it in a hurry. I sacrificed style to quickness and clarity of expression.

I didn't have time to smooth out all the rough edges, and I didn't try to. I wanted to get to the heart of the matter, and forget about flourishes of style.

If my ideas have gotten through, then I won't regret having chosen that method of working. As a matter of fact, I did have the choice between a book I would write and publish immediately, and one that would perhaps be more complete and composed in a more pleasing fashion, but published later — or perhaps no book at all.

I decided it would be more efficient to write as I did and publish immediately.

A sense of urgency on the road to sovereignty — that's what I want my readers to feel.

We might have to sacrifice a little elegance, and there's no doubt we'll leave some rough spots. But at this time in our history, I believe our choice is between quick action supported by an extremely favourable political setting, or a slower, but not necessarily better-thought-out process, which may mean we'll miss the boat altogether.

I don't think I'm wrong in saying that the people of Quebec are ready to determine their political status and future.

And I'm sure I'm not wrong in saying that it's up to the people of Quebec and them alone to make that decision.

I urge all those who support sovereignty to unite within the Parti québécois.

I also urge all my compatriots to demand that Mr. Bourassa give them the freedom to choose as soon as possible.

And I urge Mr. Bourassa once again to hold a referendum on Quebec sovereignty as soon as possible.

NOW!
NOW!
NOW!

Saint-David de Yamaska
August 30, 1990